HOW TO BEAT BURNOUT

HOW TO BEAT BURNOUT

by

Frank Minirth, M.D.
Don Hawkins, Th.M.
Paul Meier, M.D.
and Richard Flournoy, Ph.D.

MOODY PRESS

CHICAGO

All Scripture quotations, unless noted otherwise, are from the
Holy Bible: New International Version. Copyright © 1973, 1978,
1984 by the International Bible Society.

Library of Congress Cataloging in Publication Data

How to Beat Burnout.

    1. Burn out (Psychology)—Prevention.   I.Minirth,
Frank B.
BF481.H67   1986   158'.1   86-14601
ISBN 0-8024-2314-0 (pbk.)

12 Printing/BC/Year 94 93 92 91 90

Printed in the United States of America

CONTENTS

CONTENTS

ACKNOWLEDGMENTS

The authors would like to gratefully acknowledge those whose contributions helped to make this book possible.

Special thanks goes to a number of people who risked burnout to type and compile the manuscript. Those include Carol Mandt, Teresa Pakiz, Debra Stack, Jim Schneider, and Kathy Short.

Further thanks goes to Marty Williams Anderson for extensive writing and editorial work, which included coordinating the efforts of four different authors.

INTRODUCTION

While in north Dallas recently I decided to take advantage of a couple of hours' free time to pay an old friend a visit. I hadn't seen him in several years, but a mutual friend had mentioned his name to me the previous week, and I decided to look him up.

An elevator gently whisked me into the heart of a glass-and-steel skyscraper, and I stepped off into the plush reception area of a major radio station. It was quite a contrast to the Spartan central Texas studios where Bob had first introduced me to radio broadcasting.

The receptionist smiled and asked, "May I help you?" When I explained that I had dropped by to visit Bob, I was shocked by her response. Her face reacted as if she had been hit. Her voice quivered, and tears came to her eyes. Choking, she whispered, "You haven't heard?"

"What happened?" was all I could reply.

It took her a minute to form the words. "Bob is dead! A little over a year ago. We just couldn't believe it."

Several memories flashed through my mind, like slides in rapid-fire sequence. Bob's pleasant laughter when I threw the wrong switch on my first encounter with a radio control board. Pleasant mornings spent drinking coffee and discussing the ins and outs of radio production. Bob's patience in handling equipment failures. Bob and I with our wives attending a Billy Graham Crusade at Texas Stadium. The smile on Bob's face when he told me he had been appointed operations manager of a major Dallas station.

My mind replayed tapes of numerous conversations, on subjects ranging from spiritual to political to nonsensical. Still, I couldn't quite grasp the full impact of what I had just been told. After all, Bob was only a few years older than I. The last time I saw him, he seemed in prime health. What happened?

Prodding back her tears, the receptionist continued. "We really miss Bob. We still can't believe it." She went on to explain that Bob had encountered two major job failures and the breakup of his marriage, all within a short span of time.

I waited for an opportunity to phrase my question. "Did he have an accident? A heart attack?"

I'll never forget her reply: "No," she said, "Bob died of natural causes. Even the doctor said Bob just burned out."

Burnout, a term heard with increasing frequency these days, is becoming a prominent fact of life in the fast-paced and stress-filled final decades of our twentieth century. In gathering material for this book, we discovered that people in all walks of life are experiencing burnout, perhaps as never before. We have found burnout within our own families, our counseling staff, our colleagues in ministry, and in the lives of a large proportion of those people to whom we minister. Most of us have experienced some degree of burnout, at least short term, or we have been close to someone who has. All of us writing this book know what burnout is firsthand.

Except for a few such as Bob, or those who use suicide as a way of escape, most of us eventually recover from burnout to some degree.

Yet many wait too long to counter its effects or try dead-end roads to ease the strain. They end up losing their jobs, their health, and sometimes their families. They may never recover from those effects.

That is the bad news.

The good news is that there is hope for recovery from burnout. And there are warning signs that can be used to prevent you or those close to you from ever experiencing burnout. That good news is our reason for writing this book.

DON HAWKINS

1
WHAT IS BURNOUT, AND WHO GETS IT?

No one expected Catherine to experience burnout; but that's exactly what happened. Raised in east Texas, the third of four daughters, Catherine grew up in a Christian home, trusted Christ as her Savior at an early age, committed and dedicated her life to Him in junior high, and served as the president of her church youth group in high school.

During her early years, however, another drive also began developing with her. As Catherine puts it, "My sisters did well, so I felt pressure to do well, to be smart like they were." Although personable and extremely attractive—enough so to later work as a model—Catherine had a poor self-concept. "I just didn't think very much of myself; I felt the need to prove myself all the time. Even though my parents were loving and accepting, I put a lot of pressure on myself to do well. For example, in school I expected to make A's even though I wasn't an A student."

Those internal pressures hit head on with external stress in college and nursing school, where Catherine began to experience the warning signs of burnout. "There wasn't a lot of time for rest. After classes all day there was work in the hospital, and I often skipped meals and sometimes slept four or five hours a night." During that time, Catherine also started modeling to help pay bills. That added more pressure to her time schedule. "There was no time for outside activities or hobbies, just for school and work."

Soon Catherine began having trouble sleeping. She says, "I just couldn't handle the pressure. I cried a lot; my grades began dropping; I just felt exhausted all the time. When I finally finished school, I didn't want to be a nurse, or even want to be around doctors, nurses, or medicine. In fact, I didn't care if I ever took my state board exams. I graduated from nursing school a semester late, decided to forget about nursing, and went to work as a secretary. I was really burned out."

Burnout is when one's attitude becomes "a job is a job is a job," according to Edelwich and Brodsky, authors of one of the first books on burnout. To them, job burnout is when people get to the point of just putting in their time, not making waves, and just barely getting by or going through the motions.

Psychologist Herbert Freudenberger, who claims credit for the term, says that burnout is a depletion of energy and a feeling of being overwhelmed by others' problems.

According to psychologist Christina Maslach, an early researcher of the problem, burnout is "a syndrome of emotional exhaustion, depersonalization, and reduced personal accomplishment that can occur among individuals who do 'people work' of some kind."[1]

In our own experience in counseling, burnout victims show those same three factors. Feeling physically and emotionally exhausted, victims frequently cannot face the future, and they detach themselves from interpersonal closeness. Sensing themselves to be drained emotionally, they also suffer spiritually.

1. Christina Maslach, *Burnout—The Cost of Caring* (Englewood Cliffs, N.J.: Prentice-Hall, 1982), p. 3.

The detachment leads to depersonalization—looking down on people, reacting negatively to them, and developing an attitude of "I wish people would go away and leave me alone."

That attitude toward others, coupled with a feeling of emotional exhaustion—especially when seen in compassionate Christians and workers in the caring professions—results in a reduction in personal accomplishment. A feeling of diminishing accomplishment leads to stronger feelings of personal inadequacy, which further reduces accomplishment. And thus the vicious cycle of burnout is established.

A well-known business consultant believes that burnout is a major reason American industry today has such a hard time achieving gains in productivity.

THE ROLE OF STRESS

One of the most common definitions of burnout describes it as a loss of enthusiasm, energy, idealism, perspective, and purpose. It can be viewed as a state of mental, physical, and spiritual exhaustion brought on by continued stress.

Although a certain amount of stress is common, perhaps inevitable, and some stress is positive, too much stress over too long a time can result in burnout. Too much burnout, without learning and applying certain coping techniques, can lead to clinical depression. We might view this on a continuum as follows:

Stress ——➤ Burnout ——➤ Depression

Dr. Hans Selye, probably the most widely recognized authority on stress, defines stress as our body's response to any demand made upon it. He divides stress into two types: (1) *distress*—excessive levels of continued, damaging stress, and (2) *eustress*—a good, positive kind of stress one feels at times of happiness, fulfillment, or satisfaction.

Although some stress is necessary for everyday living and, in lesser amounts, even for learning and growth, large, continued (chronic) amounts of stress, even eustress, can debilitate people mentally, physically, and spiritually. We do not, therefore, want to eliminate all stress from our lives, but we do need to learn how to better handle and manage the necessary stresses of life.

BURNOUT OF THE WHOLE MAN

Too much stress and burnout affect the whole person—physically, emotionally, and spiritually. Physical symptoms can include anything from ulcers and digestive upsets to coronary problems. Often a burnout victim experiences a constant sense of fatigue, coupled with an inability to sleep. Emotionally, a burnout victim often suffers from depression. That results from being angry with oneself because of an inability to function at one's previous high performance level. Spiritually, burnout victims often reflect what could be called a "Martha complex"—extreme anxiety over proving one's self-worth by serving God and others.

That syndrome is illustrated in the gospel of Luke, when Jesus visits the home of Mary and Martha. Martha became overly involved in housework and felt her sister Mary should help her instead of sitting and listening to Jesus teach. Not only did Jesus tell Martha that her priorities were wrong, but He gently and carefully explained to Martha that, because of her anxiety over work, she was "tied up in knots" (Luke 10:41). That is the literal meaning of Jesus' original words, which can be translated "cumbered about," "anxious and bustling," "worried and bothered," or "upset." Many people can relate to Martha's anxiety in trying to prove their self-worth through their work.

Each of us is a potential target for burnout. Increasingly we find symptoms showing up in ministers, lawyers, physicians, housewives, psychologists, social workers, police officers, parents, computer professionals, nurses, industrial workers, secretaries, counselors, corporate executives, managers, missionaries, teachers, and students. Half the parents in America—according to professor Joseph Procaccini, as well as one of five ministers today—according to an Alban Institute survey—suffer burnout.

One of the tragic paradoxes of burnout is that the people who tend to be the most dedicated, devoted, committed, responsible, highly motivated, better-educated, enthusiastic, promising, and energetic suffer from burnout. Why? Partially because those people are idealistic and perfectionistic. They expect too much of themselves as well as of others. Also, since they started out performing above average, others continue to expect from them those early, record-breaking results over the long haul, even though no one would expect a runner in the one-hundred-yard dash to keep up that same speed in a cross-country run.

Burnout is:

- a parent feeling overly responsible when a child does something seriously wrong
- a missionary who uses a relatively minor health problem as an excuse for escaping the burdens and frustrations of living in a foreign culture
- a pastor, who is idealistic and overcommitted, try-

ing to please everyone in his congregation and feeling guilty when he doesn't

- a nurse in a large hospital who takes her time or even ignores a patient's buzzer request for attention
- a mental health worker who just doesn't seem to care any more
- a factory worker who goes to lunch and doesn't return
- a doctor who finds himself avoiding certain patients
- an artist sensing that his creativity is expressionless
- an alcohol rehabilitation counselor drinking more and more, while complaining about his clients who drink
- a school principal griping about her teachers
- a teacher griping about her students
- a business executive who finds himself unable to function at his previous level
- a salesman who has become so depressed that he is considering suicide
- a homemaker who finds herself in total despair after taking on too many activities

These examples are taken from cases of burnout treated in our clinic. More about these individuals, their particular symptoms, and their recoveries will be given in later chapters.

BURNOUT IN HUMAN SERVICES

Burnout is the end result of prolonged job-related or personal stress. The helping professions—nurses, doctors, pastors, social workers, and therapists, for example—seem to be particularly prone to burnout.

Why? Human services workers, who deal with other people's personal problems, are employed in highly stressful occupations.

We've encountered a psychologist who left his profession to go to work in an oil field, a social worker who left her job to open up a ceramics shop, and a teacher who abandoned his field for a sales position. All of them had one thing in common: they were dedicated people in human service professions who left their careers, not just because of salary considerations, but because they were disillusioned and headed toward burnout if they did not change their outlook or their profession.

Many people change jobs because they are burned out. Although one person left his job as a psychologist to work in an oil field, another left a stable and secure administrative position in state government with a fixed salary to join a private psychiatric clinic. Even though his monthly salary would no longer be guaranteed, he preferred practicing individual and group therapy to doing reams of institutional bureaucratic paperwork, which was leaving him increasingly frustrated and burned out.

THE THREE BURNOUT AREAS

1. *Mental.* Burnout shows up mentally in the form of a feeling of disillusionment or failure as a person or worker. Signs of anger, cynicism, negativism, or increased irritability spring up. Burnout victims may feel frustrated by a sense of helplessness, hopelessness, or self-doubt, which then may lead to depression. Another common sign is guilt—false guilt over trying to be overly responsible or committed, a feeling of not doing something perfectly or well enough. Other symptoms of mental or emotional burn-

out include apathy, difficulty concentrating or pay
ing attention, decreased self-esteem, feelings of dis-
enchantment, disillusionment, disorientation, or
confusion.

2. *Physical.* Throughout the years of our counseling, we have observed that continued stress and
burnout may bring on backaches, neck aches, headaches, migraines, insomnia, loss of appetite (or a
never-satisfied appetite), ulcers, high blood pressure,
constant colds, digestive problems, allergies, or in
the most severe forms of continuing stress and burnout, heart attacks and strokes.

In many people, unrelieved, unresolved tension
and stress result in their turning to alcohol or drugs,
either prescription or over-the-counter, for temporary
relief. The decreased energy and fatigue symptomatic
of drugs tend to worsen an already burned-out feeling.

3. *Spiritual.* Some people experience spiritual
exhaustion with burnout. Such individuals seem to
have lost perspective and have failed to recognize
their own limits. They usually experience a gradually
increasing feeling that God is powerless and that
they themselves are the only ones with the power to
help in their current situation. Without realizing
what they are doing, they refuse—consciously or unconsciously—to rely on God's power and try to play
God themselves. They may drop times of personal
spiritual meditation and Bible reading, only to feel as
if they are in a spiritual vacuum where nothing or no
one appears to be able to help. Then as time passes,
they realize that their own power, or energies, are not
enough either. They become disillusioned or feel like
giving up, believing that others, including God, have
given up on them.

Like Solomon, they may describe the advanced effects of their burnout in terms similar to this:

> So I hated life, because the work that is done under the sun was grievous to me. All of it is meaningless, a chasing after the wind. I hated all the things I had toiled for . . . because I must leave them to the one who comes after me. And who knows whether he will be a wise man or a fool? Yet he will have control over all the work into which I have poured my effort and skill. . . . This too is meaningless. So my heart began to despair over all my toilsome labor under the sun. For a man may do his work with wisdom, knowledge and skill, and then he must leave all he owns to someone who has not worked for it. This too is meaningless and a great misfortune. What does a man get for all the toil and anxious striving with which he labors under the sun? All his days his work is pain and grief; even at night his mind does not rest. This too is meaningless. (Ecclesiastes 2:17-23)

At the beginning of this chapter we learned of Catherine's experience with burnout, which parallels that of many people today. Some never recover, but Catherine did. In fact, the secretarial job she took was at the Minirth-Meier Clinic. As she describes it, "It seems God put me in just the right place to be able to recover from burnout and to ultimately become involved again in my chosen field of nursing."

And how did Catherine recover from burnout? "I first recognized that I was burned out; then I began doing something about it. I learned to take care of myself physically. I cultivated my spiritual life. I developed outside interests. And perhaps most important of all, I learned not to be so hard on myself, to allow myself to fail occasionally, and to forgive myself when I did fail."

The rest of this book is dedicated to sharing the kind of insights Catherine discovered, insights that can help individuals beat burnout. We will explore the symptoms of burnout—the warning signs—to help those who may be approaching burnout recognize the dangers before they become devastating. We will examine significant causes of burnout, including early-life factors, personality factors, stress and environment factors, and a surprisingly significant element to which Christians can be particularly susceptible.

Finally, we will discuss positive steps for reversing burnout, steps that, if taken, can make it possible for former burnout victims such as Catherine to lead healthy, productive, balanced lives.

Burnout is serious, but for those who are feeling its effects, there is hope.

2
WARNING: DOWNWARD SPIRAL AHEAD!

In the fall of 1900, a massive hurricane struck the Texas gulf coast. The city of Galveston, lying squarely in the path of the storm, bore the brunt of the hurricane winds and accompanying tidal wave. More than six thousand people lost their lives.

Today, more than eight decades later, when hurricanes roar across the Atlantic to hit the east or south coasts, only a few lives are lost. Why? Because advance warning techniques have improved vastly since the turn of the century. Now hurricane watches and warnings are widely broadcast. And people in threatened areas heed the storm warnings and evacuate to safety.

Just as meteorologists can now recognize certain signs as storm warnings of an approaching hurricane, so psychologists today can recognize storm warnings—symptoms of approaching burnout—that need to be heeded. Such warnings tend to build on top of one another. As Freudenberger notes, they involve:[1]

Exhaustion. Lack of energy associated with feelings of tiredness and trouble keeping up with one's usual round of activities are the first warning signs of burnout.

1. Herbert Freudenberger and Geraldine Richelson, *Burn-Out* (New York: Anchor, Doubleday, 1980), pp. 62-66.

Detachment. The next warning sign is putting distance between oneself and other people, particularly those people with whom one has had close relationships. People on the edge of burnout have less time and energy for relationships, since more and more of their time and efforts are concentrated on just "keeping up."

Boredom and cynicism. According to Freudenberger, boredom and cynicism are "natural companions. One begets the other; detachment begets them both." The burnout victim "begins to question the value of friendships and activities—even of life itself."

Increased impatience and irritability. Usually burnout victims are people who have been able to do things quickly. However, as burnout takes hold, their own ability to accomplish things diminishes, and their impatience grows and causes flare-ups with others. They blame family and coworkers for things that were their own fault more than the fault of others.

A sense of omnipotence. Some burnout victims may have thoughts such as "Nobody can do my job better than I," or "Only I can do it, nobody else." They may also think subconsciously—while denying it consciously—that "Not even God can do it, only me. I'm more powerful and see things more correctly than anyone, even God." Obviously, that form of exaggerated subconscious thinking, which is not unusual among burnout victims, borders on the delusional.

Feelings of being unappreciated. Burnout victims experience complex feelings of bitterness, anger, and resentment because they are not being appreciated more for their added efforts. Why not? Because those added efforts, instead of producing added results, are generating reduced results. Rather than acknowledging that, they blame others for their reduced results.

Change of work style. Reduced results and conflicts with colleagues and other work-related contacts will eventually cause one of two things to happen. Either the victim will withdraw from decisive leadership and work habits, or he or she will seek to compensate for the conflicts by becoming more and more tyrannical, demanding, or inflexible, which only causes the cycle of burnout to worsen.

Paranoia. Once burnout has taken long-term hold, it is a small step from feeling unappreciated to feeling mistreated or threatened. The advanced burnout victim may sense that someone is "out to get me."

Disorientation. As burnout continues long-term, the victim will have increasing difficulty with wandering thought processes. Speech patterns will falter, concentration spans will become increasingly limited, and the ability to remember names, dates, or even what he or she started to say will diminish. The victim may jokingly refer to having a problem of increasing old age or senility, but increasing agitation and inward stress are the problem.

Psychosomatic complaints. Physical ailments seem more conventional and therefore easier to accept than emotional ailments. The following physical complaints will flourish in the burnout victim: headaches, lingering colds, backaches, and similar complaints. These physical symptoms are frequently induced or at least prolonged by the burnout victim's emotional stress. The complaints may have real physical causes, but, more than likely, they are brought on by emotional stress, which the sufferer may not want to admit. Often, the victim focuses more on physical complaints than usual, as those become the "scapegoat," on one end of the spectrum, for the person's emotional condition and, on the other end, for the negative work results of his burnout.

Depression. There are differences between a generally depressed state and the form of depression that usually signifies burnout. In burnout, "the depression is usually temporary, specific, and localized, pertaining more or less to one area of life." The depression of most burnout victims is apt to be anger at other people for causing his or her problems.

Major depression. Some depressed burnout victims will experience major depression, a *generally* depressed state that is usually prolonged and pervades all areas of a person's life. Furthermore, the generally depressed person has turned blame for negative circumstances towards self. Instead of being angry with others, he or she tends to feel guilty for everything that is going wrong.

Suicidal thinking. As depression associated with burnout progresses, the result can be suicidal thinking. Suicide is the tenth leading cause of death in the U.S. Ten percent of individuals who make suicidal gestures eventually die of suicide. Certain personality types, such as the hysterical personality, may make suicide threats or gestures that are manipulative in nature only. However, obsessive-compulsive personalities are more likely to make actual suicide attempts.

CASE EXAMPLES

Some victims of burnout treated in our clinic were mentioned in chapter 1. Those include:

The parent who felt overly responsible when a child did something seriously wrong. A Christian mother, Mrs. A, did a reasonably good job in raising her children, as did her husband. Yet one child grew up and lived in total rebellion against God. When Mrs. A looked back on her life, she remembered circumstances in which she didn't act in the way she believed a perfect mother should have. As a result, she blamed herself totally for the child's failure. She suffered from false guilt and major depression.

The missionary who used a relatively minor health problem as an excuse for escaping the burdens and frustrations of living in a foreign culture. After several years of being a foreign missionary, Mr. B found he really did not enjoy missionary work as much as he thought he would and felt he had made a mistake. He thought he could serve God better in the U.S. in a different capacity. And yet he was embarrassed to come back and tell his supporters that he had decided not to be a missionary any more. He blamed a relatively minor health problem on his decision to return to the U.S. Then he felt guilty about using that as an excuse.

Mr. B's burnout symptoms included exhaustion from "culture shock" (which normally involves impatience and irritability when coming upon so many obstacles in a different or slower culture that make it impossible to accomplish as much as one can in one's own culture), withdrawal from decisive leadership, psychosomatic complaints (which had some basis, but relatively minor), and depression involving guilt—guilt from giving up and guilt from blaming his withdrawal on what was, at best, a half-truth.

The pastor who is idealistic and overcommitted, trying to please everyone in his congregation and feeling guilty when he doesn't. The Reverend C showed up for every meeting, for all the missionary society meetings and Sunday school meetings, and he felt guilty whenever he didn't. Whenever anyone asked him for counseling, he went ahead and saw them, even when his schedule was already full. As a result, he was ignoring his own personal needs, was not getting enough sleep, and was not spending enough time with his wife or children. He felt guilty about not spending enough time with his family, which was in danger of falling apart, and he also felt guilty whenever he said no to anyone in his congregation. Reverend C's symptoms included exhaustion, detachment (from family), and major depression (including guilt).

The nurse in a large hospital who was taking her time or even ignoring patients' buzzer requests for attention. A conscientious nurse, Miss D normally took good care of her patients. Because of her long working hours, however, and grudges she had toward her supervisor, she became clinically depressed. Her supervisor expected too much, including requiring her to work overtime too many weekends. Afraid of losing her job, Miss D said nothing about the long hours. Finally, she reached the point of losing her motivation, resulting in poor work. When she got to the point of ignoring patients' buzzers, she sought out our counseling help.

Miss D's symptoms included exhaustion, detachment (from patients), cynicism, feelings of being unappreciated, a change of work style, paranoia (fear of being fired if she requested fewer hours), depression (accompanied by anger toward her supervisor for her problems).

The mental health worker who just didn't seem to care any more. Mrs. E did a lot of counseling in a psychiatry unit. She helped many people who suffered from depression, and she loved her patients. Yet talking to people fifty to sixty hours a week about depression finally got to her. She started to get clinically depressed herself. Mrs. E's symptoms included exhaustion, boredom and cynicism, feelings of being unappreciated, and depression.

The factory worker who went to lunch and didn't return. An eighteen-year-old recent high school graduate, Mr. F had landed a factory job that paid well. At first he liked the job. It wasn't difficult, he had opportunity to meet people of all ages, and "it sure beat doing schoolwork." But spending all of his time on an assembly line, turning a screw on a part, repeating the process thousands of times a day, all day long, forty hours a week eventually began to get to him. Because of the monotony, the noise level, and the heat in the nonair-conditioned factory building, Mr. F became burned out. One day he went to lunch and didn't come back, planning to quit his job.

Mr. F's symptoms were exhaustion, boredom, feelings of being unappreciated, irritability, and depression (accompanied by anger toward those who were making him work in an undesirable work environment).

The alcohol-rehabilitation counselor who was drinking more and more, while complaining more and more about his clients who drank. For most of his life, Mr. G had not been a drinker. He enjoyed people and enjoyed working with them, but he was finding himself becoming more and more frustrated. A number of the alcoholics with whom he was working were poorly motivated and were not getting better. They would not do what they needed to do to get over their problems. That made Mr. G angry, because he wanted them to get better, both because he loved them and also because their refusal to get better made him feel powerless.

As a result, Mr G became increasingly angry and began drinking himself. The drinking brought on a greater depression, physically related, by lowering the serotonin level in his brain. He then began drinking to excess, which made him feel temporarily numb to his pain. However, the day after a drinking bout he would be even more depressed.

Mr. G's symptoms were detachment, impatience and irritability, feelings of being unappreciated, and major depression (from both physical and psychological causes).

The business executive who found himself unable to function at his previous level. A highly energetic and intelligent man, Mr. H had risen to the presidency of his company by the time he was forty. When he reached fifty, however, he was still trying to maintain the sixty-hour week that had helped carry him to the top of his company, and then maintain a multitude of outside activities as well. When he found he could no longer do all that, he began to get angry—angry at himself for getting older, angry at God for allowing him to get older, angry at the aging process itself, and angry because he was unable to concentrate quite as well. The anger brought on depression, which made his concentration level even worse.

Mr. H's symptoms included exhaustion, impatience and irritability, change of work style, disorientation (involving a lowered concentration level), and depression (related to his anger).

The salesman whose depression had led to suicidal thinking. A middle-aged man with some health problems, Mr. I, a Christian, occasionally had experienced bouts with depression over the years. After turning forty, he suffered two significant losses: his job and the impending breakup of his marriage. As a result, he had to work longer hours for less money at a job that gave him little satisfaction. His marital conflict aggravated his job-related burnout and left him with no emotional support. Mr. I's strong personal need to achieve, coupled with the hopelessness he felt concerning his circumstances, led to depression and suicidal thinking.

Mr. I's symptoms included exhaustion, detachment (from former colleagues, as well as from his wife), boredom (in a less than challenging job), feelings of being unappreciated, psychosomatic complaints, major depression (involving hopelessness and guilt for all his problems), and suicidal thinking.

The homemaker who found herself in total despair after taking on too many activities. A workaholic homemaker, Mrs. J had been the oldest daughter in her family. Her mother had been critical of her while she was growing up; no matter what she did it wasn't quite enough. Her school grades were usually A's with a few B's. Whenever she got a B, her mother criticized her. When Mrs. J married, she carried her workaholism and obsessive-compulsive desire to please into her marriage and motherhood experience. She did too much for her children, including home schooling. That allowed her to think for them, control them, and teach them herself, even though she lived in an area that had good public schools that were not offensive to Christians.

Mrs. J was active in a number of church organizations, taught Sunday school, was president of the women's missionary society, was the church organist, and sang special solos and duets. She was a workaholic career woman, even though it wasn't a paid career. As a result of her workaholism and striving to live up to her own mother's expectations of having a "perfect" daughter, Mrs. J suffered a major depression and burnout.

Mrs. J's symptoms included exhaustion, impatience and irritability, feelings of being unappreciated, change of work style, paranoia, disorientation, and major depression (accompanied by guilt from not doing everything perfectly).

All of these people, after a time spent under the care of our clinic, were able to reverse their burnout spiral and recover. Much of the information that helped them do that is shared in this book. Had this book been accessible to them, some of them would have had the information they needed to overcome their burnout without direct professional care. Others would have been helped by this information but would still have needed special care before their burnout spiral would have been reversed.

THE WORKAHOLIC—CANDIDATE MOST LIKELY

Although anyone can be subject to burnout, one personality type seems to be particularly prone to that condition. Most of the above case examples were "Type A" or obsessive-compulsive personalities. They are the ones who tend to be the most vulnerable for potential burnout. These individuals, often described as workaholics, are marked by four characteristics: (1) a hectic schedule, (2) a strong achievement orientation, (3) an inability to say no, and (4) a tendency toward frequent cardiac problems.

Such workaholic personalities often show the following symptoms of potential burnout.

The major source of self-esteem and pleasure is work and productive activity. Obviously, there is a valid amount of pleasure and self-esteem that should be received from work. However, since many people received only conditional love from their parents during childhood, when they were doing what pleased their parents, they condition themselves to feel significant only if they are being productive.

The major drive of obsessive-compulsive or workaholic individuals is a need for achieving control. That includes a need to control self, others, circumstances, and one's environment. (For a detailed list of characteristics of the obsessive-compulsive in dividual, as well as reasons behind these, see *The Workaholic and His Family* by Minirth, Meier, Wichern, Brewer, and Skipper [Grand Rapids: Baker 1981].)

More than 90 percent of physicians and 75 per cent of ministers who have been tested through the Minirth-Meier Clinic lean primarily toward these obsessive-compulsive personality traits. Many of these may tend to "play God" over their staff or congregations, refusing to delegate control over even the least significant responsibility or problem.

THE SPIRITUAL ELEMENT

A lack of spiritual "daily bread" often compounds the burnout victim's self-efforts. Often, when one feels the pressure of burnout, the first thing to be eliminated is the time for personal reflection, meditation, and spiritual devotion. The pressures of a busy schedule, coupled with an increasing inability to keep up, crowd out a time for meditating on the Word which is essential in keeping a sharp edge spiritually, mentally, and physically. Rather than meditating on

Scripture, burnout victims often spend that amount of time worrying about the problems that are pressing in on them.

Perhaps, then, decreased times of spiritual devotion should be the first warning sign of a potential burnout victim. And since surveys show that only 5 to 10 percent of Christians practice daily times of Bible study and meditation, at least 90 percent of Christians should be considered more susceptible to burnout than they would be otherwise.

One successful businessman and Sunday school teacher, who was headed toward burnout, told us, "I realized that the shortened amount of time I was spending in the Word was being used only to find things to feed my class. All the while, I was starving spiritually and needed to feed myself. I decided that it was necessary, for a time, to give up my Sunday school class and spend time in the Word just feeding myself."

One sign of good mental, emotional, and spiritual well-being is a sense of day-to-day and moment-to-moment dependence upon God's enabling power for self and for others.

When individuals begin to experience burnout, one warning sign is an increasing sense of self-effort. Rather than trusting God or even others' God-given abilities in particular circumstances, burnout victims simply try harder, thinking they must depend more and more upon self. Interestingly, when committed Christians start depending more on themselves, they may start giving more lip service to their trust in God in order to cover up their decreased dependence on Him.

The classic example of that is seen in Moses' experience with the children of Israel during their years in the wilderness. There in the desert, God told

Moses to "speak to that rock" and water then would come out of it to refresh the Israelites. Weary and disgusted with the Israelites complaints about desert living, his leadership, and God's ability, Moses took credit for the rock's life-giving water, not by speaking to it but by striking it twice with his rod. Moses' statements to the congregation, "Listen, you rebels, must *we* bring you water out of this rock?" (Numbers 20:10, italics added), showed that he thought his efforts were needed on top of God's abilities to get the job done.

In verse 12, God reprimands Moses for that action. "Because you did not trust in me enough to honor me as holy in the sight of the Israelites," He denied Moses the right to lead the Israelites into the Promised Land, because He considered Moses' usurping of His own glory, in front of His people, reprehensible.

That example alone should be enough to cause a person in the burnout spiral to take heed when attempting to do God's work in personal strength alone. Trusting God for His inexhaustible provision of energy and enablement, either through self or through others, is not only the true practical way to handle a situation, but it is the way God wants it in order that His glory and power, instead of one's own, is demonstrated to others.

A TIME FOR ACTION

The time for taking action to break the downward spiral of burnout is at the first recognition of any storm warnings. Remember, burnout is a reversible spiral. The key is to begin action immediately to take care of oneself and to reverse the burnout.

God wants us to have peace. The Old Testament word *shalom* ("peace," a common Jewish greeting) is a term that indicates far more than simply the absence of hostility. It includes that (Joshua 9:15), but on a more positive note it suggests also a quality based on a strong relationship (Psalm 41:9; Jeremiah 20:10). That relationship leads to tranquility or contentment, which is one of three component parts of biblical peace (Psalm 4:8; Isaiah 32:17). It also includes the element of recompense, restoring, or making complete (1 Samuel 24:19; Joel 2:25). Finally, and most significantly, the biblical concept of peace includes completion. In fact, that is the basic concept of the Old Testament root word for peace. This is beautifully illustrated in the use of the word in 1 Kings 7:51 regarding Solomon's completion of the Temple.

How does that relate to us? God's will for the Christian is to experience the legacy of peace that Christ left for his followers. "But the Counselor, the Holy Spirit, whom the Father will send in my name, will teach you all things and will remind you of everything I have said to you. Peace I leave with you; my peace I give you. I do not give to you as the world gives. Do not let your hearts be troubled and do not be afraid" (John 14:26-27).

He wants us to experience tranquility, contentment, the absence of inner strife, and completeness. We must take steps to reverse burnout's downward spiral in order to fulfill that aspect of God's will. Inward peace of mind, plus fullness and abundance in life, is the will of God for Christians (Isaiah 26:3; Philippians 4:6-7).

Jesus said, "Come to me, all you who are weary and burdened, and I will give you rest" (Matthew 11:28). Those dedicated workers who consciously and without apology stop to take good care of themselves mentally, physically, and spiritually, will have, by far, the best chance of eventually fulfilling their life's purpose and calling. Theirs will be the experience of peace.

BURNOUT INVENTORY

If you believe you are headed for burnout, here is a way to test yourself for symptoms of a downward spiral ahead. Check those statements with which you agree.

1. More and more, I find that I can hardly wait for quitting time to come so that I can leave work.
2. I feel like I'm not doing any good at work these days.
3. I am more irritable than I used to be.
4. I'm thinking more about changing jobs.
5. Lately I've become more cynical and negative.
6. I have more headaches (or backaches, or other physical symptoms) than usual.
7. Oten I feel hopeless, like "who cares?"
8. I drink more now or take tranquilizers just to cope with everyday stress.
9. My energy level is not what it used to be. I'm tired all the time.
10. I feel a lot of pressure and responsibility at work these days.
11. My memory is not as good as it used to be.
12. I don't seem to concentrate or pay attention like I did in the past.
13. I don't sleep as well.
14. My appetite is decreased these days (or, I can't seem to stop eating).
15. I feel unfulfilled and disillusioned.
16. I'm not as enthusiastic about work as I was a year or two ago.

17. I feel like a failure at work. All the work I've done hasn't been worth it.
18. I can't seem to make decisions as easily as I once did.
19. I find I'm doing fewer things at work that I like or that I do well.
20. I often tell myself, *Why bother? It doesn't really matter anyhow.*
21. I don't feel adequately rewarded or noticed for all the work I've done.
22. I feel helpless, as if I can't see any way out of my problems.
23. People have told me I'm too idealistic about my job.
24. I think my career has just about come to a dead end.

Count up your check marks. If you agree with a majority of those statements, then you may be feeling burnout and be in need of professional help or counseling or, at least, a change in life-style.

3
UNFULFILLED EXPECTATIONS: THE BURNOUT BURDEN

Burnout involves unfulfilled expectations, being worn down and tired out because what one thought would happen hasn't come about. Unfulfilled expectations relate basically to rewards that were expected but not received, rewards such as happiness, praise, attention, a sense of satisfaction, or a sense of well-being or security.

Often, unfulfilled expectations occur because those expectations have been too high. If you lower your expectations to more realistic ones, you are less likely to burn out. (Of course, if you lower them to the point that you want to "just forget the whole thing," you are already in burnout.)

But shouldn't Christians have high expectations? Oh, yes. We should expect God to work miraculously, but in His way, not ours. As Jeremiah learned: " 'For my thoughts are not your thoughts, neither are your ways my ways,' declares the Lord. 'As the heavens are higher than the earth, so are my ways higher than your ways and my thoughts than your thoughts' " (Isaiah 55:8-9).

Often a Christian's high expectations are not a reflection of God's thoughts so much as they are attempts to be involved in God's work in the world, in order to get praise from others (including the Lord) as a boost to one's own ego or shaky self-esteem. Sometimes the high expectations even started off from a right base, only to change their foundation later on.

In Romans 12:3, we are told: "Do not think of yourself more highly than you ought, but rather think of yourself with sober [sound] judgment, in accordance with the measure of faith God has given you." That doesn't mean you should not think of yourself highly, as someone God died for, but "not . . . more highly than you ought," not as if you are indispensable. Often, one approaches or experiences burnout because of the thought, "If I don't do it, no one else will," or "No one else will do it right." That is indeed thinking of self more highly than one ought to think. God has resources, as good as, if not better than, the ones He has given us, to complete a job (if He wants it done), resources that we know nothing about.

ELIJAH'S UNFULFILLED EXPECTATIONS

Certain events in the life of the prophet Elijah read like a modern-day case study in burnout, because of his unfulfilled expectations. In his interaction with Queen Jezebel, following his great victory over the prophets of Baal and his subsequent flight to the wilderness, Elijah exhibited many symptoms characteristic of what we today call burnout. A study of the events in 1 Kings that surrounded that interaction shows why he suffered that condition and what God did about it. Applying that divine "wellness program" to your life can start the reversal of your own burnout spiral.

In considering that and other passages of Scripture, it is important to distinguish between interpretation and application. Interpretation deals with what the specific passage means in its historical context to the individual or people to whom it was written. Application, on the other hand, has to do with the significant or relevant principles that can be drawn from the passages concerning life today.

Nearly a thousand years before Christ, Israel was ruled by the wicked king Ahab and his equally wicked queen, Jezebel, who had spread the worship of Baal throughout Israel. During these dark days, Elijah's character and ministry surfaced like a bolt of lightning, in startling contrast to the life-style of most Israelites. His words were characterized by boldness, his ministry by miraculous deeds. His commitment and willingness to stand for the true God of Israel, as well as his dependence upon Him, are illustrated in a challenge to the 450 prophets of Baal to a competition of miracles and in his prayers, for fire and, a short time later, for rain. One would think that an Elijah would never suffer burnout. However, Elijah was no super-human individual. As James 5:17 explains, Elijah was "a man just like us."

Elijah, in fact, is a vivid biblical example of Freudenberger's observation that burnout "is the letdown that comes in between crises or directly after 'mission accomplished.' "[1] Elijah was successful, a high achiever. He expended a great deal of physical, emotional, and spiritual energy in his conflict with the prophets of Baal in front of the Israelites gathered on Mount Carmel. His success caused the Israelites and their king to come back to the worship of the only true God. Shortly after that incident, he expended more energy by climbing to the top of Mount Carmel, spending an intense period of time in prayer for rain to end a three-year drought and, when that prayer was answered, running twenty miles from

1. Herbert Freudenberger and Geraldine Richelson, _Burn-Out_ (New York: Anchor, Doubleday, 1980), p. 110.

Carmel to the city of Jezreel. In his excitement and in the power of the Lord, he even outran King Ahab's chariot.

Following all these strenuous but miraculously successful activities, Elijah received an unexpected jolt: Jezebel swore that she would have him killed. Expecting more success, he was instead rejected and threatened. His heady joy was replaced by fear. He turned and began running again, this time for his life, to Beersheba in Judah. And then, leaving his servant behind, he walked or ran for another day into the desert.

After courageously confronting 451 of his enemies—King Ahab and the prophets of Baal—why would he turn and run at a death threat? Instead of persisting in prayer, as he had done for rain (1 Kings 18:41-45), why did Elijah flee?

Existing on a physical and emotional high at that point, he had been caught off guard emotionally and spiritually. With the adrenaline still flowing, he depended upon the strength that had brought him to Jezreel, physical strength. So instead of praying, he ran.

ELIJAH BURNS OUT

As he ran from Jezreel to Beersheba for his life, he must have become more and more depressed, more and more burned out physically. That is easy to understand. Emotionally, his expectations of Jezebel had not been fulfilled. Spiritually, he had exchanged his dependence upon God for what little physical strength he had left. Compounding the problem, he abandoned his servant, withdrawing to the wilderness alone. With no close friend or associate, no one to help or encourage him, he was overcome by feelings of despair and self-pity. Note carefully in 1 Kings 19:3-4 the emotions experienced by Elijah as he came to a broom tree, sat down under it, and prayed that he might die. " 'I have had enough, Lord,' he said. 'Take my life; I am no better than my ancestors.' Then he lay down under the tree and fell asleep."

Elijah felt detached and isolated from everyone. The focus of his thinking was on himself. He was obsessed with a desire to be more successful than his ancestors. Setting and seeking to reach unrealistically high standards led to Elijah's burnout and frequently leads to burnout today.

Note how Elijah's self-centered thinking continued even forty days later, after God had given Elijah rest and food, and even insight, through the question recorded in 1 Kings 19:9-10: " 'What are you doing here, Elijah?' He replied, 'I have been very zealous for the Lord God Almighty. The Israelites have rejected your covenant, broken down your altars, and put your prophets to death with the sword. I am the only one left, and now they are trying to kill me too.' "

ELIJAH'S BURNOUT SYMPTOMS

A cluster of feelings associated with burnout find their expression in these verses. They include:

1. *Egotism.* Elijah's egotism was associated with feelings of being indispensable. Ultimately, God reminded the prophet that he was not the only one left, that there were still seven thousand who had not worshiped Baal. At that stage, however, Elijah felt that he was the only one. His sweeping generalization of Israel's apostasy was only partially accurate.

2. *Feelings of resentment and bitterness.* He resented the fact that others had abandoned God. And

his bitterness within drained away important emotional energy.

3. *Feelings of paranoia.* The prophet says, "And now they are trying to kill me too." It would seem that he had expanded one death threat into a national crusade to assassinate him.

4. *Feelings of self-pity.* Note the "I" emphasis in Elijah's words.

5. *Feelings of resentment and anger toward God.* Certainly, God did not need to be reminded of how zealous Elijah had been for His name. Asking God to take his life (v. 4), coupled with the complaint, "They are trying to kill me" (v. 10), demonstrated his dissatisfaction and lack of trust concerning God's supreme control over his life, as well as a desire to have personal control over when his life ended.

All these feelings are likely to be experienced by an obsessive-compulsive individual who feels burned out. Since "Elijah was a man just like us," it is easy to see how a study of his burnout case can give insight into coping with burnout today.

GOD'S REMEDY FOR BURNOUT

Observing God's compassionate dealings with Elijah can give us principles that we can apply in handling burnout today.

First, He met Elijah's physical needs—rest and then nourishment (vv. 5-6).

Second, God allowed Elijah to see that He still remained in control of circumstances and was still active in the prophet's life. The extended communication between the two of them (vv. 9-17) demonstrates God's continued concern for the prophet.

Third, during that communication, God prompted Elijah to ventilate his intense feelings. To get rid of negative feelings, it is important not to bury them but to express them (although not in a manner hurtful to others, which only compounds problems for both parties).

When we expose our feelings to others, only then can we begin to see them realistically—for what they are—and then to get rid of them. Often, however, an extended period of time is necessary for those feel ings to come to the surface and dissipate. So it was, with Elijah, as God patiently prompted him three times to open up and state how he felt (vv. 4, 10, 14)

Fourth, only after Elijah had exposed his feelings did God give him new but lighter tasks. God assigned Elijah a series of tasks that he was capable of han dling—anointing two new kings and a new prophet (vv. 15-16). An individual who has experienced burnout should not be rushed back into situations involving major stress. However, taking on lighter tasks that can be handled more easily helps rebuild the self-esteem of the burnout victim.

And finally, God provided for Elijah something every burnout victim needs after his recovery: a genuine friend. From that point on, Elisha became Elijah's friend, fellow worker, and disciple (vv. 18, 21). Elijah had come to feel that he was alone. Those feelings, of course, did not reflect the true situation, since seven thousand other Isralites had also refused Baal worship. On the other hand, Elijah had been alone, but only because, like many burnout victims, he had brought about his own aloneness by abandoning other people (his former servant and others in his flight to the wilderness.)

To summarize, God reversed Elijah's "burnout" by meeting his basic needs. Elijah needed rest and nourishment, which He provided. He needed fellowship with God, so God spoke to him through "a gentle whisper" (v. 12). Elijah needed a proper perspective of himself—a sense of self-worth—so God assigned him a task he could handle. Finally, the prophet needed close relationships with others, so God provided his friend and servant, Elisha.

Elijah, the successful high achiever, was almost at the peak of total success. He had been miraculously victorious in all his endeavors. All he needed was Jezebel's conversion to the true God, which he may have anticipated was at hand, to experience total success in his pursuits for God. When the major crisis was over, the main part of his mission accomplished, he dropped his spiritual guard, expecting smooth sailing. Instead, his expectation regarding Jezebel not only was unmet but was turned against him. When he saw that his expectations were to be unfulfilled, burnout came quickly, because he had exerted his physical and emotional resources to their limits, and he no longer trusted in his spiritual strength.

So it is with us when we expect success because of our own efforts and within our own time limits. When expectations are unfulfilled, whether those that were originally God-given or not, and we start depending less on God and more on ourselves, burnout is not far behind.

4

BITTERNESS: A HIDDEN ROOT

In our Christian psychiatric clinic, two women, Lucy and Linda,* were treated for suicidal depression. Both of them came from similar backgrounds. Although they grew up in different parts of the country, both were oldest daughters raised in Christian families active in the church. Both Lucy and Linda began participating in their church's music program at an early age and continued to do so after they were grown. Both were also involved in teaching.

Yet soon after becoming adults, both became severely depressed to the point of being unable to function. Lucy, in fact, had developed multiple personalities. Each came to our clinic as the result of strong suicidal thoughts.

After months and even years of treatment, both began making significant progress. Lucy ultimately became healthy and functional. Linda, however, continued to struggle.

In examining the similarities and differences between these two women, one key factor became evident. Both women had been sexually and emotionally abused by their fathers and by other male family members at an early age. For years, both had blocked out that repeated abuse from their conscious minds.

*Names have been changed.

When compassionate Christian counselors enabled them to remove the blocks that had led to their severe depression, consciousness of what had happened to them came to the surface.

When they became aware of what had happened, however, their responses were somewhat different. Over a period of time, Lucy chose to forgive her father and others for what had happened. Linda, on the other hand, retained a measure of bitterness and resentment. She continued to harbor feelings of anger and resentment and could think or talk of little else. As a result, her process of healing and restoration was severely hampered.

Both Lucy and Linda had experienced severe burnout as wives and mothers. However, one was able to recover and experienced restoration from burnout. The other did not experience the same measure of recovery. Why? Because of the relationship between bitterness and burnout.

In our counseling ministries, we have seen literally hundreds of examples that verify a close connection between bitterness and resentment and the experience of symptoms that we call burnout. The purpose of this chapter is to give a biblical perspective on bitterness, to show how bitterness leads to burnout, and to show how freedom from bitterness is necessary for effective recovery from burnout.

Sometime ago, one of our staff was speaking at a regional pastors' conference in the Midwest. A number of the pastors attending the conference expressed their enthusiasm when they discovered that the theme of the messages would be burnout. However, several pastors expressed surprise when the speaker drew attention to the connection between burnout and bitterness. As one pastor said, after the conference, "I've been feeling burned out for some time. I always thought of it in connection with serving the Lord and working hard in my ministry. I never thought part of my burnout resulted from being bitter or resentful toward the demands placed on me in ministry or towards several board members who had attempted to have me fired many years ago."

The word for *bitter* is used in both the Old and New Testaments for either a literal bitter taste or an attitude. For example, in Exodus 15:23 the Israelites attempt to drink "bitter" water. The same concept is used in illustrating a product of the heart in James 3:11: "Can both fresh water and salt (bitter) water flow from the same spring?" In a contrast between water that is bitter or brackish to the taste and that which is sweet, drinkable, and thirst-quenching, the term for bitter is used in a figurative sense of strong, negative emotions in both the Old and New Testaments. For example, Job asserts, "Even today my complaint is bitter" (Job 23:2). In Esther 4:1 the Israelites cry "loudly and bitterly." In a similar vein, Peter, after denying Christ three times, "went outside and wept bitterly" (Matthew 26:75; Luke 22:62).

One of the fundamental lessons learned in medical school is that fever indicates the presence of an infection. Therefore, simply to treat a fever without looking for its cause—the infection—is failing to practice good medicine. In reviewing the period of Israel's history between the Exodus from Egypt and the arrival of the new desert-raised generation in the Promised Land, Israel on several occasions demonstrated a characteristic that is related to bitterness in the same way that fever is related to infection. That characteristic, far from being outdated, is prevalent today even among many Christians. It is referred to in Scripture as "murmuring" or "grumbling" (in whispers).

Although each of us has had extensive Bible training, including seminary degrees, none of us, until recently, had ever heard or read a word study on "murmuring." As we begin examining that term, we discovered that, with the exception of a reference in Joshua 9:18, all occurrences of the word *murmuring* were found in six chapters of Moses' two books: Exodus 15-17 and Numbers 14, 16, and 17.

We discovered also that the term is always followed by the preposition *against:* "murmured against." The subject of the verb, to murmur, was always the congregation Israel: "Israel murmured against." The object of the murmuring was usually an authority figure, either Moses or Aaron. At times, Moses alone was the object of murmuring (Exodus 15:24; 17:3). At other times, the Lord was the object of murmuring (Exodus 16:7-8; Numbers 14). As we examined that concept, we discovered that there was always some external reason for murmuring—bitter water, not enough food, or dissatisfaction with the decisions made by those in authority.

What is murmuring? Our definition for murmuring is to express resentment, dissatisfaction, anger, or complaint in low or half-muted tones. Murmuring is the opposite of unconditional obedience. It also stands in stark contrast to grateful trust. Our definition includes several component parts.

First, it involves opposition expressed in muted but audible tones. The Israelites' murmur against Moses and Aaron in Numbers 14:2: "If only we had died in Egypt! Or in this desert!" Although the passage infers that the Israelites communicated their murmuring to each other, it nonetheless was audible to and directed against Moses and Aaron and, ultimately, God.

In our teaching careers on the college and seminary level, we frequently witness murmuring because of an unexpected quiz or of an announcement of a difficult assignment. In fact, during our own student days, each of us engaged in murmuring. Another component of the biblical concept of murmuring is hostile opposition. In fact, in Numbers 14:9 Moses describes the nation's murmuring as an act of rebellion "against the Lord."

A third component of murmuring is that it constitutes unbelief. The Lord so labels the Israelites' murmuring in Number 14:11: "How long will these people treat me with contempt? How long will they refuse to believe me, in spite of all the miraculous signs I have performed among them?"

Sometime ago, the wife of a man engaged in full-time Christian ministry came for counseling about the pressures under which her husband labored. During the course of her initial conversation, she observed, "I really don't have any problems myself." However, she expressed complaints about several people in church, a couple of her office colleagues, and even about some incidents that had occurred in her family years before. During the counseling session, she asserted that both she and her husband were "burned out."

It took some time to demonstrate to her the connection between her feelings of burnout and her bitterness toward the people and incidents about which she had complained.

Murmuring is a common phenomenon today and is present in the lives of many of us who are Christians, including those who have experienced burnout.

Second, we are observing that, as fever indicates the presence of infection, murmuring can show the underlying presence of bitterness.

Few passages illustrate that relationship better than Exodus 15. The Israelites, under Moses' leadership, successfully crossed the Red Sea. They witnessed the miracle of deliverance from the Egyptian Army, then sang, under Moses' direction, a great hymn of praise to God for that deliverance.

Only three days after singing the words, "Who . . . is like you, O Lord?" (v. 11), they found themselves three days' journey into the wilderness without water (vv. 22-24). Coming to a place called Marah, they discover water. However, it was too bitter and distasteful to drink. Their response? "The people murmured against Moses, saying, What shall we drink?" (KJV).

That response to adversity—murmuring—was repeated numerous times during Israel's years in the wilderness. However, in that first incident, we discover a clue that demonstrates the connection between murmuring and bitterness. Exodus 15 does not say that the people were bitter, yet the name of the location in which Israel is first said to engage in murmuring is Marah, which means *bitter*. It seems unlikely that the Holy Spirit, in directing Moses to record these words, left us with the name of that obscure location by accident or without purpose. It seems that God went to great pains to point out the bitterness of the water. And we believe that was to highlight the underlying bitterness of the people.

Another factor present in Exodus 15, which is frequently connected with murmuring and, consequently, with bitterness, is a short memory. Just three days earlier, the Israelite nation had been electrified by the magnitude of God's deliverance. Now, it seems, they were complaining, "God, what have you done for us lately?"

In much the same way, a graduate student received a sizeable gift in the mail that enabled him to pay for almost an entire semester of studies. Less than two weeks later, he was bitterly complaining about his financial circumstances because he was not able to take his wife out to eat regularly.

In Psalm 103:2 the psalmist writes, "Praise the Lord, O my soul, and forget not all his benefits." Perhaps one of the most effective ways to reduce the possibility of burnout in our lives is to remind ourselves frequently of both the big and small ways that God "daily loads us with benefits" (Psalm 68:19, NKJV*).

THE CAUSES OF BITTERNESS

1. *Wrong motives or jealousy.* In counseling Christians, we frequently see bitterness associated with jealousy. The examples include successful attorneys who envy the abilities of their colleagues, Bible college and seminary students consumed with jealousy toward fellow students whom they perceive as having more insight into Scripture, and pastors or missionaries envious of others who have seen more outward evidences of success in their ministries.

2. *Wrong response to irritations; conditional love.* In Colossians 3:19 Paul instructs husbands to "love your wives, and be not bitter against them" (KJV†). The Greek word *pikroi* used here demonstrates "resentment or an incensed and angry attitude of mind." Frequently, we hear wives assert, "Nothing I do ever pleases him. I can't cook, can't keep house, can't take care of the children, or can't balance the checkbook to please him." Sometimes we

*New King James Version.
†King James Version.

hear husbands in marital counseling making the same assertions. One husband even used such assertions to justify his having an affair with another woman. His rationale? "I'm not sure I love her any more."

We believe that kind of bitterness and petty criticism often results from an underlying lack of unconditional love. Unlike God, we often are guilty of having *conditional* love, based on the performance of the one we supposedly love. Conditional love produces harshness and bitterness both in husbands and wives. Frequently, that can lead to marital burnout. However, conditional love and marital burnout can be reversed.

3. *Wrong response to adversity.* In Hebrews 12:15, we discover a warning that "no bitter root grows up," instead of enduring "hardship as discipline" (v. 7). Although not all adverse circumstances are direct acts of divine discipline (e.g., Satan's attacks on Job to get him to disavow God, "When [God] has tested me, I will come forth as gold" [Job 23:10], all adversities are designed to produce a proper response that leads to growth in grace and knowledge of God. As 2 Corinthians 4:17 tells us, "For our light and momentary troubles are achieving for us an eternal glory that far outweighs them all."

In calling for a proper response to circumstances of discipline, Hebrews 12:14 requires a response of peace with all men and *holiness* in our relationship with God. If we fail to diligently pursue these qualities, bitterness may take root. As that bitterness grows and develops, often beneath the surface of our conscious thoughts, it becomes more and more a part of our outlook on life. The results are devastating, both to us and to those around us.

4. *Misplaced strife.* James 3 provides a good illustration of the literal and figurative uses of the word *bitter* in the New Testament. In verse 11, bitter or salt water is used as an illustration of bitter conversation. In verse 14, the underlying attitude in the heart is demonstrated. In that section, James is calling for a demonstration of wisdom through meekness. However, when jealousy and selfish ambition are present in the heart, it often leads to strife, which in turn presents "disorder and every evil practice" (v. 16).

We have seen churches that for years have been crippled in their effectiveness for Christ because of "bitter envying and strife" on the part of church leaders. Even missionary and other organizations composed of Christian leaders are frequently rendered less than effective because of petty jealousies. In one local church, one of the elders, motivated by jealousy, refused to recognize the good job other leaders were doing and sought to disqualify every candidate but himself from the upcoming church election. He was unable to see his own bitterness until his pastor lovingly showed him how he, too, could be disqualified.

5. *An unforgiving spirit.* Often in counseling we hear about insults or offenses that have occurred years before. Sometimes we hear the words, "I just can't forgive." Invariably, when we hear those words, our response is to encourage our counselee to insert the more accurate word, "I *won't* forgive." Forgiveness is always a choice. Like love, it involves an act of the will.

Ephesians 4:31-32 draws a clear connection between bitterness and what is perhaps its most basic underlying cause, a refusal to forgive. "Get rid of all bitterness, rage and anger, brawling and slander, along with every form of malice. Be kind and compassionate to one another, forgiving each other, just as in Christ God forgave you."

That passage connects bitterness with underlying anger, outbursts of temper, ill will, and evil speaking. The contrast in verse 32 shows how conflict, anger, and unkindness are so frequently related to a refusal to forgive.

It is in that passage, and specifically in verse 31, that we see the ultimate solution to bitterness. The choice to which Paul calls believers who have been wronged is clear. First, we must choose to *put aside* or *get rid of* all bitterness and associated anger, outbursts of temper, ill will, and unkind words. Frequently, bitterness will grow and develop for years simply because we nourish it by talking about those offenses that have occurred. We voice our hurts to anyone who will listen and often to those who would rather not. In quiet moments, rather than meditating on Scripture, we spend our time meditating on those hurtful moments and how we felt.

EXPRESS ANGER APPROPRIATELY

Bitterness and its underlying emotion, anger, is unhealthy. Repressed anger needs to be appropriately and properly expressed. That's why earlier in Ephesians 4 Paul says, "In your anger do not sin: do not let the sun go down while you are still angry" (v. 26). If we are angry with our mate, with other Christians, with a family member, with our neighbor, or with a colleague at work, we should confront those persons, if at all possible, and carefully and lovingly express our feelings before the sun goes down (or before the day is over). To do otherwise is unhealthy spiritually, mentally, or physically.

CHOOSE TO FORGIVE

The second choice we must make is the choice to forgive. That choice first involves an approach of kindness and tenderheartedness. Frequently, we have seen individuals who, having been injured in the past, develop what might be called "a hard edge." They become calloused and insensitive to the feelings of others, or even to their own need for relationships with God and with other people. That hardened emotional state is often difficult to reverse.

Our pattern for forgiving is none other than Christ Himself. "Be kind and compassionate to one another, *forgiving each other,* just as in Christ God forgave you" (v. 32, italics added). The words of His prayer from the cross come vividly to mind: "Father, forgive them, they do not know what they are doing" (Luke 23:34). Peter, who experienced Christ's forgiveness firsthand, reminds us of how Christ, "when they hurled their insults at him, he did not retaliate; when he suffered, he made no threats. Instead, he entrusted himself to him who judges justly" (1 Peter 2:23). Surely, none of us have suffered wrongdoing to the extent of that suffered by our perfect and holy Savior.

What then is forgiveness? The word itself means to send or put away. It does not necessarily mean that we will forget. Frequently, forgetting is impossible, because the hurt has become burned into our long-term memory. However, we can choose to maintain consciousness of harmful events, or we can choose to do as Christ did and act as if they had not occurred. Forgiveness is a matter of the will; it is a choice. Furthermore, when we choose to forgive, we relieve a great deal of the ongoing mental and emotional stress that is required for nursing grudges. As a result, we are far less susceptible to burnout.

Elizabeth was a pastor's wife. For years she gave herself to her husband, her children, and the various churches and individuals to whom they ministered. Over a period of years, the ministry began to take its toll. There were times when her husband was less than sensitive about her physical and emotional needs. Church members were frequently harsh and critical, especially toward her husband and children. Yet, many of those same people often demanded hours and hours of her time. Elizabeth soon became burned out.

A change in her husband's schedule, followed by a move to another ministry, helped some. However, it was not until Elizabeth consciously *chose* to forgive a number of people—including her husband and children—and expressed a willingness to give up the bitterness that she admitted she felt that she began to actually recover from burnout.

We are far more likely to overcome burnout if we *choose to forgive* rather than choose to hold on to bitterness.

5

THE WORKAHOLIC AND HIS WORKPLACE

When most people hear the word *burnout*, they think of the hard-driving business person who never stops for coffee breaks or relaxing lunches, and who insists on taking work home at night, or even on vacations. There are, of course, occasional situations where such a workstyle is necessary. If that workstyle has been practiced long term, however, its necessity is as much in the mind of the workaholic as in the reality of the situation.

Seemingly logical explanations of, "That's the only way to get the job done," "That's the only way to get ahead in my profession (or company)," or "We need the extra money," are all too often cover-ups for the feeling, "That's the only way to prove to them what I'm worth," which ties in with the feeling, "That's the only way to prove to *myself* and others what I'm worth."

Many times a workaholic will try to make a virtue out of his overdependence on work (for a feeling of self-worth) by exalting work, the "Protestant work ethic," and even capitalism, to a far higher plane than in the mind of God. We are in favor of all three but not in order to excuse someone's destructive workaholic habits.

Work itself certainly is not to be shunned or downgraded. The apostle Paul knew that when he said:

We were not idle when we were with you, nor did we eat anyone's food without paying for it. On the contrary, we worked night and day, laboring and toiling so that we would not be a burden to any of you. We did this, not because we do not have the right to such help, but in order to make ourselves a model for you to follow. For even when we were with you, we gave you this rule: "If a man will not work, he shall not eat." (2 Thessalonians 3:7-12)

However, workaholism for the purpose of glorifying or exalting self is unnecessary and wrong, just as it was wrong for the Tower of Babel to be built "to the heavens," in order to "make a name for ourselves" (Genesis 11:4).

WORKAHOLISM AND GUILT

To verify the rightness of their workaholic tendencies, strong obsessive-compulsive individuals point out that whenever they slow down, they feel guilty for not accomplishing all that they *should* be doing, or even all that they believe God gave them the ability to accomplish. Yet, nowhere does God say that it is His will to carry out work that causes us to neglect Him, our families, and our health.

That unnecessary guilt or false guilt, felt whenever workaholics slow down, may be related to an anxiety regarding their fear of facing what had *not* been accomplished during their times of frenetic workaholic activity, things such as spending time with God, with family, and improving one's own mental and physical health. Also, many of the accomplishments of workaholics later on are found to be all for nothing, because not enough time was spent in planning and prioritizing for long-term accomplishment. To the workaholic, everything seems extremely important and urgent at the time.

One burnout victim, president of a fairly large company, told us the harsh realization that all his work was not what the Lord had in mind for his life had come slowly. God instead wanted him to work at being successfully balanced in work and family life. Allowing himself to become one-dimensional and obsessed with work, even to the detriment of everything else in his life, had seemed like a good quality to have previously. Now, however, he saw it for the selfish sin it was.

OBSESSIVE-COMPULSIVE PERSONALITY TRAITS

That executive's personality, such as that of all workaholics, is heavy with obsessive-compulsive personality traits, some good and some bad.

To discover whether or not your personality is primarily obsessive-compulsive, which may make you susceptible to workaholism and eventual burnout, see if a majority of the following traits apply to you.

1. is perfectionistic, neat, clean, orderly, dutiful, conscientious, meticulous, and moral.
2. does a good job but works too hard and is unable to relax.
3. is choleric, overly conscientious, overly concerned, inflexible, has an overly strict conscience and rigid thinking.
4. rationalizes to deceive and defend self and intellectualizes in order to avoid emotions.
5. is a good student, well organized, and interested in facts and not feelings; seems cold and stable and tends to split hairs.
6. is anti-authority at times and is pulled between actions of obedience and defiance. Obedience

usually wins, but occasionally defiance wins. The obedience leads to rage and the defiance leads to fear. The fears lead to perfectionistic traits and the rage leads to non-perfectionistic traits. A basic problem is defiant anger.

7. displays many opposite traits: conscientiousness and negligence, orderliness and untidiness.

8. has three central concerns: dirt (he or she is very clean), time (he or she is punctual), and money (he or she wants a feeling of security).

9. has feelings of helplessness, needs to be in control of self and others who are close to him or her, needs power, and is intensely competitive.

10. keeps emotions a secret from others, feels with the mind (is too logical), and, as a defense, isolates feelings from whatever he or she is experiencing.

11. has other defenses including: magical thinking—thinking he or she has more power than reality dictates; reaction formation—adopting attitudes and behavior that are opposite to the impulses the individual consciously or unconsciously harbors; and undoing—unconsciously acting out in reverse some unacceptable action that occurred in the past.

12. struggles to bring conversations around to the level of theories.

13. is afraid of feelings of warmth (which occurred in dependent relationships in early life), expresses anger more easily (because it encourages distance), postpones pleasure (out of unconscious guilt), lives in the future, lacks spontaneity, and is insecure.

14. may have unspontaneous and routine sex with little variety. Female perfectionists have difficulty with orgasm and male perfectionists some-

times have difficulty with premature ejaculation. That is a result of anxiety, which is related to their fear of loss of control.

15. usually had a parent or parents who were obsessive and demanded total devotion but gave minimal love, and who made the person feel accepted on a conditional basis (only when doing what the parent wanted him or her to do).

16. often leans, theologically, toward an extreme Calvinistic position, in which God chooses who will be saved and the individual's own actions, even the action of freely choosing to be saved, means little or nothing. (That is because he or she has a longing for some control in his or her uncertain world, as well as a desire to avoid personal responsibility.) Emotionally, however, he or she feels like an Arminian, not good enough to warrant God's continuing salvation.

17. needs respect and security.

18. craves dependent relationships but fears them at the same time.

19. needs to feel omnipotent and substitutes feelings of omnipotence for true coping.

20. has trouble with commitment, fears loss of control, and frequently focuses on irrelevant details.

21. often uses techniques to conceal anger, such as shaking hands frequently with a handshake that is rigid.

22. has feelings of powerlessness and avoids recognition of personal fallibility. He or she fears the possibility of being proved wrong, so lives in much doubt about personal words and actions. Even door latches are checked and rechecked to achieve certainty and security.

23. is extraordinarily self-willed, uses his or her defense mechanisms to control aggressive impulses,

and avoids real conflicts by dwelling on substitute obsessive thoughts. If these defense mechanisms do not work, the result is depression.

24. is stubborn, stingy (with love and time), frugal, persistent, dependable in many ways, and reliable.

25. has an overdeveloped superego, feels comfortable only when knowing everything, and tends to insist on ultimate truth in all matters.

26. has exaggerated expectations of self and others.

Our alcohol-rehabilitation counselor, Mr. G, was just such a person. He expected to cure his alcoholic patients and he expected them to do what was necessary to be cured. When that didn't happen, he had to admit that he wasn't perfect, which to him was to be contemptible (see number 29). He received some psychiatric help, quit drinking himself (following his own advice), and resolved his anger and frustrations. He came to realize that when dealing with alcoholics, some of them will respond and want to get over their problem and will do very well, and some of them will not. He came to accept his limitations and realized that the responsibility for his patients' recovery was really on their shoulders, not on his. His responsibility was to point out to them what they needed to do and then to leave it up to them whether or not to obey God and to work out their problems. As a result, Mr. G returned to his work and was able to function well without feeling burned out.

27. appears strong, decisive, and affirmative, but is not; rather, he or she is uncertain, uneasy, and wavering. Rigid rules are followed to control uncertainty. He or she needs to appear perfect.

28. exaggerates the power of personal thoughts.

Words (spoken or unspoken) become a substitute for responsible action.

29. has a grandiose self-view and strives to accomplish superhuman achievements to overcome insecurities. To that person, accepting one's limitations amounts to being average—and contemptible.

Our case example, Mrs. A, the mother who felt overly responsible when a child rebelled against God, had just such a grandiose self-view. She thought the success of her children depended upon her alone. When one child rebelled, she not only blamed herself but saw herself as less than a perfect mother, one with limitations and therefore contemptible. That self-view brought on depression and burnout. She didn't realize that every child is born depraved and that all parents make mistakes in parenting. Mrs. A was encouraged by our staff to quit carrying all the guilt and blame for her child's wrong choices.

That is not to say that parents should overlook their parenting mistakes. They should ask God for forgiveness for their mistakes, pray for their grown children, encourage them to commit their lives to Christ, and love them unconditionally, whether or not they accept Christ. Then they need to turn the burden for their grown child's future success over to their child.

30. is cautious in love relationships, because love results in concern about another's feelings that are not under one's own control.

31. has a single-minded style of thinking, is good at tasks that require intense concentration, and believes that everything is either black or white, completely right or completely wrong.

32. has a tendency to respond to extremes.

33. is critical but cannot stand criticism.
34. has strong rituals in his or her personal religious system. Rituals are considered important in many other areas of life.
35. considers commitment tantamount to dependency and being out of control. Marriage commitment is difficult; coexistence is preferred.
36. lives in the future, saves for a tomorrow that never arrives, discounts limitations of time, and denies death.
37. insists on honesty in marriage, which results in telling all, at times.
38. has trouble admitting mistakes.
39. uses excessive cautions or restraints in courtship.
40. gives minimal commitment in relationships but demands maximal commitment. As a result, each marriage partner pursues his own interests, and intimacy is limited. He or she is careful to *do* only a minimal share in marriage but wants to *think* for both self *and* spouse.
41. is legalistic in dealing with himself and others.
42. is (a) pecuniary—obsessed with money matters, (b) parsimonious—frugal or stingy, and (c) pedantic—overly concerned with book knowledge and formal rules.

THE WORKAHOLIC'S INNER VOICES

Inner "voices" or convictions are what keep workaholics going. They tell workaholics, who are usually the oldest children of their sex in the family, that they need to do something to be worthwhile. These voices or convictions do not let him or her rest in just *being* someone. *Doing* is the key to being worthwhile.

The cause usually lies in unrealistic expectations for a first child by parents who try to get the child to *do* or accomplish new activities before a child could normally accomplish them. That is partly out of anxiety—to be sure the child is normal—and partly out of parental pride—to improve their own self-esteem through raising an above-normal child. By the time a second child comes along, these desires and anxieties have been somewhat satisfied and the parents are more realistic about what to expect from a child at different stages. Meanwhile, that first child grows up with the following inner voices that drive him on.

1. *Voice from childhood.* That unhealthy voice or driving message says, "You're a nobody. What can you do to prove you're a somebody?" When the workaholic then starts to do something to prove self-worth, the voice says, "Keep doing more, more." When the workaholic reaches a goal, the voice says, "That's good, but it's not enough." Workaholics never reach the point of doing enough to prove that self is a "somebody" and relax in that knowledge.

The only way workaholics (or anyone else, for that matter) can truly prove they are somebodies is to accept the fact that *God sees them as somebodies*—so much so that He gave His only Son to die so that He could fellowship with them eternally. True self-worth can be experienced only as we understand and acknowledge our position as *accepted* or *acceptable* to Jesus Christ, because we claim, for ourselves, the payment that He made for our sins by dying on the cross.

2. *Voice of the depraved self.* That voice says, "I'll do what I want to do. I'll have fun or do my own thing." That conviction, reinforced by Satan, comes

into dominance when the workaholic out of exhaustion gives up on the first voice—in other words—when he is approaching burnout. The burned-out workaholic may still be going to work in order to receive a paycheck, but he or she is no longer exerting as much effort.

3. *Voice of colleagues.* That inner voice, also unhealthy, says, "Don't take time off; you can't afford it. People won't understand." Actually, that voice may or may not be the actual thoughts of the workaholic's colleagues, but only what he or she assumes colleagues would say. To overcome that voice, the workaholic must consider what are his or her actual priorities in life and in the particular task at hand.

When new therapists are hired at the Minirth-Meier Clinic, we caution them (1) that the number of cases they have affects the profit the clinic makes as well as their own salary, but (2) if their case load becomes so heavy that it is affecting their home life, they are to call a halt to accepting new cases. Those priorities must be recognized and followed daily.

4. *Voice of reality.* Another voice that workaholics and all of us hear, at times, will be the voice of reality, a healthy voice that we all need. That voice tells us to "face the music" and realize that mounting debt or some other problem means that we will need to work harder or longer or a particular period of time. When that period of time is up, however, we will again need to slow down to a normal pace. The problem with workaholics, however, is that when a crisis is over they keep finding more reasons to continue the extra exertion and long hours.

5. *Voice of the Holy Spirit.* That voice, which all Christians have, says, "What does God want you to

do?" In order to hear that "still, small voice," however, the workaholic must recognize its authority over all the other voices inside and separate what it is saying from the urging of the other voices. To do that, the Christian workaholic must continually stay familiar with the basic guidelines God sets down for all Christians in His written Word.

Our case example, Mrs. J, the workaholic housewife, illustrates how a workaholic can change from listening to the voice from childhood to the voice of the Holy Spirit.

After a month of hospitalization, Mrs. J was cured of her workaholism and depression by becoming aware of her anger toward herself and forgiving herself for not being perfect, and by becoming aware of her anger toward her mother for expecting her to be perfect and forgiving her mother for not being a perfect mother. After that, she and her mother actually became better friends. She learned to see her mother as a human being, one with good traits and bad traits. She learned to be just herself with her mother, even when her mother was demanding or was giving her occasional "guilt trips" or rejection. She learned not to accept those and to choose not to feel guilty when her mother displayed such actions. She left her mother's guilt trips go in one ear and out the other and learned to enjoy her mother instead.

Mrs. J also asked God to show her her own "light and easy yoke." She decided to put her children in the local public school, which was a good one, and continue teaching Sunday school, a ministry that she enjoyed. She gave up her job as church organist, sang only occasionally, and spent more time with her husband and children sharing their basic feelings with one another. Mrs. J became a better wife, mother, person, and witness for Christ, as a result of reorganizing her priorities and reprogramming her mind to listen to God's Holy Spirit rather than to her mother's parental injunctions.

CHECKLIST FOR WORKAHOLIC BURNOUT

If you have been wondering about your own tendencies toward workaholic burnout, see how many of these four statements you agree with. True or false:

1. I feel that the people I know who are in authority are no better than I am.
2. Once I start a job, I have no peace until I finish it.
3. I like to tell people exactly what I think.
4. Although many people are overly conscious of feelings, I like to deal only with the facts.

It is interesting that several of these statements would be considered good qualities to have in an employee. However, they are actually tendencies of a person susceptible to early burnout. Following are the reasons a person is likely to agree with these statements.

I feel that the people I know who are in authority are no better than I am. Burnout includes an underlying cynical attitude and a rebellion against authority figures. That attitude revolves around one's expectations not having been met.

Once I start a job, I have no peace until I finish it. If you will work day and night until you finish a job, it not only shows that work comes before everything else, but it may be related to authority rebellion as well. It could be tied in with an *"I'll* show him!" attitude or with a boss giving unrealistic time limits and demands. It may also be tied in with an idea that "if I can just get that project put into a nice, neat little package, it will show *him* (and *me*) that I'm a worth-while person."

I like to tell people exactly what I think. As workaholics become more burned out, they become more irritable and more likely to say anything without holding back, because so much is pent up inside that there is no room to store more. Also, the more burned out, the more omnipotent and right they feel about personal viewpoints. As growing insecurity about decreasing abilities mounts, the victim becomes more arrogant. "I am right and everyone else is wrong!" Just as Jeremiah 17:9 said, "The heart is deceitful above all things."

Although many people are overly conscious of feelings, I like to deal only with the facts. If you take the emotional part of a workaholic's personality away, you would notice no difference. A workaholic represses feelings (except for irritability, and he or she doesn't recognize the basis for the irritability).

These four questions are the first in an inventory we give to suspected workaholic patients.[1] Complete the rest of this inventory as quickly as possible. Your first response is often your most honest answer. True or false:

5. I worry about business and financial matters.
6. I often have anxiety about something or someone.
7. I sometimes become so preoccupied by a thought that I cannot get it out of my mind.
8. I find it difficult to go to bed or sleep because of thoughts bothering me.

1. Presented first in *The Workaholic and His Family,* by Frank Minirth et al. (Grand Rapids: Baker, 1981), pp. 23-26.

9. I have periods in which I cannot sit or lie down—I need to be doing something.
10. My mind is often occupied by thoughts about what I have done wrong or not completed.
11. My concentration is not what it used to be.
12. My personal appearance is always neat and clean.
13. I feel irritated when I see another person's messy desk or cluttered room.
14. I am more comfortable in a neat, clean, and orderly room than in a messy one.
15. I cannot get through a day or a week without a schedule or a list of jobs to do.
16. I believe that the man who works the hardest and longest deserves to get ahead.
17. If my job/housework demands more time, I will cut out pleasurable activities to see that it gets done.
18. My conscience often bothers me about things I have done in the past.
19. There are things that I have done that would embarrass me greatly if they become public knowledge.
20. When I was a student I felt uncomfortable unless I got the highest grade.
21. It is my view that many people become confused because they don't bother to find out all the facts.
22. I frequently feel angry without knowing what or who is bothering me.
23. I can't stand to have my checkbook or financial matters out of balance.
24. I think talking about feelings to others is a waste of time.
25. There have been times when I became preoccupied with washing my hands or keeping things clean.

26. I like always to be in control of myself and to know as much as possible about things happening around me.
27. I have few or no close friends with whom I share warm feelings openly.
28. I feel that the more one can know about future events, the better off he will be.
29. There are sins I have committed that I will never live down.
30. I always avoid being late to a meeting or an appointment.
31. I rarely give up until the job has been completely finished.
32. I often expect things of myself that no one else would ask.
33. I sometimes worry about whether I was wrong or made a mistake.
34. I would like others to see me as not having any faults.
35. The groups and organizations I join have strict rules and regulations.
36. I believe God has given us commandments and rules to live by, and we fail if we don't follow all of them.

Now go back and count the number of statements you answered "true," including the ones you agreed with of the first four statements. A score of 10 or less reflects a fairly relaxed person. A score of 11 to 20 is average. A score of 21 or more reflects a definite tendency toward workaholism. If you scored in the twenties or beyond, you are also likely to become a victim of burnout.

"FACTS ONLY" THINKING ENCOURAGES BURNOUT

Unfortunately, the business world today makes a virtue out of "facts only" type of thinking. Most graduate business programs teach the student to use the "scientific method" alone in solving business problems, using only facts and logic. That means the emotional side of the employee, as well as of the supervisor, is totally ignored. We agree with a well-known executive management consultant's assessment that if business would deal with the emotional side of an employee, the whole person, the business would have a much more productive worker.

In his consulting business, this man deals with how clients and their employees are feeling. He says that too often business and industry take great employees and continually push them to make increased productivity levels until they burn out and start producing less and less. When that happens, industry usually thinks that they'll simply fire them and hire replacements. However, statistics show that it takes about two years to get a new employee to the point of productivity of an established worker. He recommends that, instead of firing employees who are not producing well, it is more productive to find a niche for them that is better suited for their personality strengths. That means paying attention to the way employees feel about and relate to the world around them. That policy is one followed by Japanese businesses, which today are experiencing a far higher productivity average than are American businesses.
productivity average than are American businesses.

CARING FOR THE WHOLE WORKER

Another policy followed in Japan is that no one works after hours and employee exercise periods and other breaks are adhered to strictly. Psychiatric studies have proved such workstyles are superior to those generally followed in American business, where employees are much more susceptible to burnout.

An example from this consultant's own experience, one with an ironic twist, validates that thinking. He was working for a Fortune 500 company, where all the other junior executives came early, stayed late, and always carried home briefcases filled with papers to work on at night. He, however, worked only regular hours and, although he took home a briefcase every night just to let everyone know he wasn't shirking, there was never anything in it!

He had already realized that competing with many others to become an officer of the company wasn't a worthy goal. Spending a half-hour in the Word every morning, he was seeing what priorities were all about, that life on earth is like the snap of a finger compared with life eternal. As he is fond of saying, "The only things you're going to be able to take into eternity with you are your spouse and children."

As a result, he concentrated on the Lord, his family, and his health outside of regular office hours. He then showed up every morning at work feeling rested and ready to put his all into his job during the regular work day. He laughs when he goes on to say that he was then given one of the first promotions among the junior executives, with a bonus of an extra week's vacation. Why? Because his superiors were sure he must be spending too much overtime on his work in order to accomplish as much as he did!

his work in order to accomplish as much as he did!

There are numerous examples of biblical characters—Joseph, Daniel, Nehemiah—who spent time with God every day and who, as a result, were among the top in the business worlds of their day. God wants people with a balanced life-style to be able to show the world that He is in control. For some, that will mean that He will see to it that they will reach the top and be able to do a good job from that position. For others, of course, He will have a simpler position in life from which they can glorify Him best.

When workers are young, it is easy for them to work hard, fast, and long and not spend time to pause and reflect on what they are doing. They hope that work pace will get them the prestige and prosperity they want in their career within a certain number of years, at which time they hope to be able to sit back, relax, and enjoy life and their families. Meanwhile, their health deteriorates and their families desert them, either physically or emotionally, for families can't wait all those years for satisfactory relationships. In his later years, the president of a large, successful, construction company in the Midwest, often said, "Slow down and take time to think. I wish I had done that when I was young, instead of working fifteen to twenty hours a day."

Another company president, Mr. H, our case example, also learned the value of slowing down and accomplishing more. When he received our psychiatric help, he came to realize that, at age fifty, there were certain things he should not be able to do as well and as rapidly as he could at thirty, but there were other things that he should be able to do better. He accepted his physical limitations but was made aware that he was now a lot wiser than he was at thirty. At fifty he should be using his wisdom and experience to bring success to his company rather than his "elbow grease."

So Mr. H cut down to a thirty-five-hour work week and began accomplishing a significant amount of good through decision-making and learning to delegate more to people under him. In fact, his company did better, and so did his family, after he slowed down to thirty-five hours a week than it had done when he was working sixty hours a week.

That proves another point that is counter to the thinking of most workaholics and burnout victims. No one is indispensable. There are other people who can do their jobs, or at least part of their jobs, as well if not better than they can. That doesn't mean the burnout victim isn't needed. It means only that he or she can be more successful in a more concentrated area while using much less energy.

As Howard Hendricks, professor at Dallas Theological Seminary, says "When you play the game of climbing the ladder to success, you may reach the top and find that, all the time, the ladder was resting against the wrong wall." Almost always, family members who take the time to enjoy one another and the simpler things in life, even if they have to sacrifice materialistic niceties to do so, are happier than those who are bringing in more money but have to sacrifice time with one another.

Of course, there are times when career transitions may make it necessary to work harder or longer for several months or so, but even then, a time limit should be set on how long one will continue to keep up such a pace and ignore or give lesser attention to other important areas of life.

One area of burnout experienced by too many today is that involving the start of a new business venture. Often, a new entrepreneur will work day and night to make a new venture profitable in a shorter amount of time than is needed. The time constraint usually has to do with financial considerations. Not enough money was available at the beginning of the venture to keep it afloat for the reasonable amount of time needed to start turning a profit. A word of warning might be to make sure enough money has been saved or raised before entering a new venture, rather than burning yourself out trying to make the new venture profitable in too short a time.

LOOKING FOR EMPLOYEE BURNOUT

An employer or supervisor may suspect burnout when an employee exhibits frequent absenteeism, more indecision, and less attention to personal grooming and health. The Monday "blahs" or blues may be an indication of approaching burnout. Of course, by the time the Monday "blahs" last all week long, the employee is in the midst of burnout. If the burnout victim is a supervisor, he or she should realize that burnout symptoms probably exist in those that report to him or her, as well. The supervisor should consider what can be done to encourage employees to want to come to work. It may include changes in reporting relationships, in office environment, and in allowing employees to have a say in the best way to accomplish projects.

Often, the relationship between employee and supervisor is to blame for burnout. The employee, if unable to change the relationship with the supervisor, should still ask, "What purpose for the Lord do I have in this job?" Often, the strains of the situation may be endured more easily when we know that God has a purpose for our being in that particular place at that particular time.

As for our nurse case example, Miss D (who was working overtime too much and was ignoring patients' buzzers), therapy helped get in touch with the anger she had toward her supervisor. After that she was able to be more helpfully assertive and not fear her supervisor's wrath or power. She let her supervisor know that she could not function working that many hours. Miss D told her that she either had to work a forty-hour week or find another job, and her supervisor agreed to allow her to work a reduced schedule. Through therapy, learning to forgive her supervisor, and cutting down her work schedule, Miss D was able to overcome her burnout and, again, become an important part in the healing of her patients.

GOD'S WILL FOR THE WORKAHOLIC

The crux of the consideration for Christians who don't want to burn out may be to consider if they are in the job God has for them. If you think you'll be fired if you spend sufficient time with family and on rest and relaxation, then it is unlikely that it is the job God has for you. Before quitting the company, however, it may be fruitful to consider if there is another type of position in the same company that would suit you better. One young Christian accountant in a large company realized that his chosen career was giving him little opportunity to deal with people on a personal level. Because he needed such contact, he asked to be switched to the human relations or personnel department of the company as a trainer. Today, he has won many awards for his innovative work efficiency programs and methods of motivating factory workers.

When we put God, family, and work in any other order, we have diminished our faithfulness to God and are saying, "I don't trust God to meet my needs." God would much rather we have less income and a more enjoyable life-style. If you quit the road to burnout, you may indeed face the possibility of being fired. However, you may be surprised to find that your rating in the company will go up instead of down, as you enter each day fresher and more ready to give your best to producing during the part of the day that should be allotted to work.

One former burnout victim and workaholic, a company chief executive officer, uses the following checklist to get his life in balance.

1. Realize that you don't have to be perfect to be "somebody." You are already "somebody" in Christ because He says you are.
2. Realize that you don't have to be completely neat in order to have other people and yourself approve of you.
3. Look at life from the eternity perspective. What will you take with you?
4. Learn to relax with activities that are relaxing to you.
5. Get in touch with your hidden anger, then forgive others for their part in it, and forgive yourself for having it.

Learning a new way of life comes hard for a workaholic, but it is necessary. A workaholic has to practice being relaxed, practice saying no to others' expectations of him, schedule time with God, schedule eight hours of sleep, and schedule time with family. The alternative is to become progressively less productive and of less benefit to loved ones and to himself as a result of burnout.

6
BURNING OUT FOR GOD

Some of the prime candidates for burnout are those people who want to serve the Lord "full-time" with all their heart, soul, and mind. Christians in vocational ministry often find themselves on the edge or in the depths of burnout. Among young, zealous Christian workers, the desire to "burn out for God" is often considered even an admirable trait and goal. The realities of carrying that goal long term, however, can be disastrous personally and to a ministry.

Several years ago, at a pastors' conference, one minister bragged to his colleagues, "I haven't taken a vacation in ten years. The only time I take off is a day once or twice a year." He then laughed at the warnings of his colleagues about keeping such a schedule. The next year at the pastors' conference, the news was passed around that that pastor was no longer in the ministry. He had suffered a physical and emotional collapse.

Another Christian worker, Jan Markel, wrote a book about her experience. She explains that she became so ministry-oriented she "was determined to serve God full-time, at least eighty hours a week."[1] As a result, she came close to suffering permanent physical damage.

1. Jane Markell and Jane Winn, *Overcoming Stress* (Wheaton, Ill.: Victor, 1982), p. 24.

The desire to burn out for God can be a costly one, for that is not what He calls us to do. Too many Christian workers burn out long before their time, spending only half a career or less in Christian service. If they continue in vocational ministry, often a long recovery period is needed before they begin to feel effective again. As one ministry-burnout victim explained it, "The usual problem with burning out for God is that you don't burn *out,* you just burn *down* to a flicker. Then you spend frustrating months and even years doing nothing but sputtering or flickering for God."

BURNOUT HABITS START EARLY

The seeds for that kind of problem, according to Dr. Archibald Hart, are usually planted during the first few years of one's career, when ministry habits and work styles are formed.[2] With a lot of textbook knowledge, hope, and untried faith, new pastors straight out of seminary or Bible college tend to look upon their calling idealistically. They believe they can solve immediately—with the flipping of Scripture pages—any and all problems they confront.

When reality proves them wrong, they continue striving to solve all problems, even though the amount of effort needed is much greater than what they had anticipated. Too late they realize that instead of doubling up their work efforts in order to keep their idealistic goals, it would have been better to have tempered their goals and recognized that *solving* other people's problems is not their calling. Being a *part* of the solution is all they are called to do. God will also use other people plus the Holy Spirit's

2. Archibald Hart, *Coping with Depression in the Ministry and Other Helping Professions* (Waco, Tex.: Word, 1984), p. 14.

leading in the life of the hurting persons to solve the problem.

Dr. David G. Congo surveyed ministers in thirty-two denominations in thirty-eight states to discover the significant factors involved in ministry burnout. His study isolated a number of significant factors involved in burnout.[3] Of the pastors surveyed:

- 70 percent worked more than sixty hours per week.
- 85 percent spent two or less evenings per week at home.
- 75 percent spent less than one evening a month purely for social time with their wives and other couples.

With such schedules, it's no wonder that many pastors experience burnout because they "grow weary in well-doing."

Of course, two other factors in ministry burnout include (1) working with a lean staff because of tight financial restrictions, and (2) everyone expecting Christian workers to put their all—heart, mind, body, and soul—into their work, since it is "for" God. Christian workers have to evaluate the work and opportunities that come to them with the question, "Is that what the Lord wants me to do at this time, or am I doing it just because it *seems* like such a great opportunity and need?" What the Lord leads you to do is not always the same as what you want to do *for* Him, especially if you are doing it in order that He or others might be more pleased with you, or that He or others might remain pleased with you.

3. David G. Congo, "What Causes Burnout?" *Theology News and Notes*, March 1984, p. 7.

Many people end up on the mission field because they see "the great need," and assume "the need is the call." That point of view is even stressed in some mission societies, often ones that have a high dropout and burnout rate. That may well have been the problem with Mr. B, our missionary case example, who had been overwhelmed by the responsibilities and cultural differences on the mission field. Instead of using his minor health problem as an excuse for leaving the field, we encouraged him to prayerfully consider where he personally could serve God most effectively and then make arrangements to do that. Mr. B decided that he could serve God better in the U.S. as an associate pastor of a church, concentrating on counseling, at which, we assured him, he was gifted.

To relieve the guilt caused by exaggerating his health condition, he was encouraged to tell his financial and prayer supporters the truth of his mission field problems and that his physical health was not the decisive factor in his leaving the field. We told him that he might experience some hostility from a few supporters, but that most of them would welcome his honest openness with appreciation and would encourage him in his future ministry even more. And that is just what happened.

ON CALL FOR BURNOUT

The sense of being constantly "on call" is another major factor in ministry burnout. Ministry workers are almost constantly in contact with the sick, the hurting, the poor, the distressed, and the dying. Frequently, one crisis call is interrupted by another, with little time in between for recuperation. Many have described to us that sick or anxious feeling that occurs whenever the telephone rings, that sense of, "Well, who or what is it this time?" which may indicate approaching burnout.

Frequently, a feeling of indispensability accompanies these constant demands. People assume that they cannot face or overcome their problems unless they have personal help from their pastor. Sometimes, those to whom Christian workers minister initiate that thinking. Most commonly, however, it is the Christian workers themselves who generate that thinking in others. One pastor, feeling that he was becoming burned out, asserted, "I can't trust any of my staff members to take care of our people's problems." Since that pastor also communicated those feelings to his people, it's no wonder that they all tended to come to him directly.

As we mentioned earlier, more than three-fourths of the ministers tested through our clinic lean primarily toward workaholic, obsessive-compulsive tendencies. Work and productive activity are their major source of feelings of satisfaction and significance. Since they formed that attitude in early childhood communications with their parents, they assume their heavenly Father, too, is satisfied and pleased with them only when they are busy *doing* something *for* Him. They have inherited the "mantle of Martha," who was tied up in knots over much serving, rather than assuming the easy yoke of Christ that was meant for them.

THE DRIVE FOR CONTROL

The workaholic's main drive is a need for *achieving control*. Thus, workaholic ministers, as much as they would deny it, tend to "play God" over their congregations, often refusing to delegate control over even the least significant responsibility or problem. When instructed to delegate, they may *assign* control to others, but they then will insist on keeping on top of every detailed effort of the assignee.

Or, if one small assigned project is done to less than their own standards, they will usurp the authority they have given, take over the project themselves, and bemoan, "It seems I'm the only one who can get the job done." They refuse to see that God may be working in the other person's life, allowing him to learn from his mistakes in order to do better the next time, or if someone else needs to take over, it shouldn't be themselves.

BALANCING THE BURDEN BEARING

David Congo's pastoral burnout survey also showed that 61 percent of pastors spend less than one hour a week talking with other pastors.[4] A second key factor, then, can be observed from Congo's survey. Besides becoming burned out because they "grow weary in well-doing," many pastors receive little support from their peers in similar occupations.
pations.

The demands on a pastor often makes it difficult to carve out time to spend with fellow pastors, yet time so invested can be invaluable in keeping them from burning out. That situation is often even more acute in the case of foreign missionaries, who may find geographical, cultural, and financial barriers to peer fellowship and support. The difficulty comes when they allow the ever-increasing pressures of more to do and less time in which to do it to crowd out time when they and other fellow servants of

4. Ibid.

Christ could be "bearing one another's burdens." Such loners often reap the harvest of their failure to sow seeds of mutual support. Frequently, that harvest will involve burnout.

John D. Carter and Janelle Warner studied a selected group of Presbyterian pastors, their wives, and church members, to assess the differences in loneliness, marital adjustment, and vocational burnout. Their conclusion was that both pastors and pastors' wives experienced significantly more *loneliness* than those in non-pastoral roles, and that pastors' wives experienced higher levels of *emotional exhaustion* than non-pastoral males and females. Thus their statistical survey substantiated the premise that burnout is related to a lack of support.

According to the Carter/Warner study, "The pastor and his wife . . . spent less time together because of the demands of their efforts in Christian service. Subsequently, they may begin psychologically to withdraw from each other and from friendships due to burnout; he being overly involved and she being emotionally exhausted. As a result, they experience loneliness and less marital satisfaction."[5]

Christian workers know that the Creator has established certain fundamental laws upon which things operate. They don't try to defy the law of gravity or assume that, if they refuse to recognize it, it won't operate. However, they often try personally to defy or to refuse to recognize God's principle of sowing and reaping. They may teach it to others, putting great emphasis on Galatians 6:7, "Do not be deceived: God cannot be mocked. A man reaps what he

5. John D. Carter and Janelle Warner, "Loneliness, Marital Adjustment and Burnout in Pastoral and Lay Persons," *Journal of Psychology and Theology*, Summer 1984.

sows." They fail to recognize, however, that in Galatians 6 the apostle Paul is relating the principle of sowing and reaping to the *imbalance in carrying each other's burdens.*

Paul explains how Christians should function in relationship rather than in isolation.

> Brothers, if someone is caught in a sin, you who are spiritual should restore him gently. But watch yourself, or you also may be tempted. Carry *each other's* burdens, and in this way you will fulfill the law of Christ. If anyone thinks he is something when he is nothing, he deceives himself. Each one should test his own actions. Then he can take pride in himself, *without comparing himself* to somebody else, for each one should carry *his own load.* (Galatians 6:1-5, italics added)

In the process of explaining the overall implications of spiritual sowing and reaping in connection with other people, Paul shows a knowledge of what today we call burnout. He exhorts us to "carry [bear] each other's [heavy] burdens," in order to help Christians who have fallen into sin regain spiritual health without being tempted to sin again (because of having to carry too heavy a load).

To *disperse* and *balance* the carrying of one another's loads within the Christian community, Paul also urges us *not* to carry *too much* of others' burdens. "Watch yourself, or you also may be tempted" (v. 1). Then he warns against the opposite extreme—allowing others to take on too much of *our own* responsibilities. "Each one should carry his own [light or manageable] load" (v. 5).

Then, in verse 9, Paul brings the sharing of burdens exhortation and its accompanying principle of spiritual sowing and reaping to bear on symptoms that we know to be involved in burnout. He states,

"Let us not become weary in doing good, for at the proper time ["in due season," KJV] we will reap a harvest if we *do not give up*" (italics added).

The implications of that verse for burnout sufferers is obvious. First, they become "weary" in doing good. Pouring themselves into the quest for accomplishing more and more, they are overcome by exhaustion. They take increasingly less and less time for having personal, physical, and spiritual needs met.

LOSING ONE'S PERSPECTIVE

That leads to the second factor, they lose their long-term perspective, unable to see that "in due season, we shall reap." They sacrifice the future on the altar of the present.

An example of that second factor is Ed, a dynamic young Bible college graduate, who had overcome a speech impediment, and who was called to serve as pastor of one of only two Bible-teaching churches in a medium-sized city. At first, things went well. However, after several months, Ed discovered the existence of deep divisions in the church body. The harder he tried to heal those divisions, the more he discovered that the people on both sides turned against him. He and his wife became the targets of frequent criticism, which led to further discouragement. Hours and hours of meetings with the various factions failed to do anything but deepen the divisions.

After less than two years in the pastorate, Ed gave up, even though two fellow pastors had encouraged him to "hang in there." As one of the church leaders put it shortly after Ed's resignation, "He had already been through the worst of it; in fact, things were about to turn around. We probably would have lost one more family and, I think, after that, there would have been harmony." Unable to see that his persistence was about to pay off, today Ed is out of the ministry, divorced from his wife, and selling insurance.

GIVING UP

Ed's case also illustrates the third factor isolated for us by the apostle Paul in Galatians 6:9. He simply gave up. Paul says, "We will reap . . . *if we do not give up*" (italics added). Giving up is the culmination of the burnout process Paul described for us in Galatians 6:9. The process begins with *doing well,* but as well-doing escalates, we *become weary;* we then *lose the perspective* of "reaping in due season" and, ultimately, we "faint" or give up.

REVERSING MINISTRY BURNOUT

Please note that the answer is not to cease doing well. It is the contrary. Paul explains in verse 10, "As we have opportunity, let us do good to all people, especially to those who belong to the family of believers."

WORK FOR NEED, NOT APPROVAL

Often, the problem arises when we go beyond opportunity, endeavoring to gain the approval of self, God, or others on a performance basis. In his survey, Congo observes that some pastors have personality tendencies that make them more vulnerable to burnout. These are pastors who "have a high need for approval, pastors who derive their self-esteem from their work, pastors who are unassertive and feel controlled by others, and pastors who believe that the only way a job will be done right is if they do it themselves.[6] That, he says, answers the question why in a given church one pastor burns out and another thrives.

According to Congo, one way to avoid burnout is, "Turn the rat race into a relay."[7] His suggestions mirror the principles articulated by the apostle Paul in Galatians 6:9. One involves not trying to do it all yourself. Certainly, in that context, Paul's emphasis on bearing one another's burdens is one often overlooked by pastors who consider themselves the bearer of burdens for all those to whom they minister and who consider it inappropriate to share their own burdens with others. Those patterns, obviously, are prime candidates for burnout.

One of us found that true in his own ministry. His workaholism was all right while he was in college, graduate school, medical school, and during a hospital residency in psychiatry. But then he began experiencing burnout. His main symptoms were exhaustion and anger. His worst experience was when he was teaching pastoral counseling in a seminary, carrying on a part-time private practice, counseling students at home at no charge, taking theology courses, and speaking at seminars nearly every weekend. He said yes to every chance to minister.[8]

He then would read in Matthew 11:28 that God's "yoke is easy and his burden is light." That verse, he said, made him angry because he thought God's burden was overwhelming. Then he began to see that not all his burdens were from God. Many burdens he had taken on were a result of his own insecurities

6. Congo, p. 7.
7. Ibid., p. 8.
8. For further information see the introduction from *The Workaholic and His Family*, by Frank Minirth et al. (Grand Rapids: Baker, 1981), p. 13.

and subsequent desire to please everybody.

At that point, he learned to prioritize things better, to put his own relationship with God first, his family next, and his work or ministry third. That took several years to bring to complete reality. Now, instead of saying yes to everybody, he says no most of the time. When his schedule gets to the point of being a full "light" burden, then he says no to everything else, in order to keep time for his family.

A sidelight to his decision was that, at first, he had the following negative results:

1. He felt false guilt over not doing as many things as he had previously, when he thought that God wanted him personally to "rescue the world for Christ." He realized that if he personally were to try to meet every need he saw, he would soon be only one more needy person. Occasionally, he still feels a twinge of false guilt, however, when he can't meet others' demands or expectations.
2. He received hostility from other Christians, who were not used to his saying no (or who didn't think he should) to requests to minister to specific needs, to serve on boards, or to attend Christian meetings.
3. As he cut his work load from seventy-five to forty hours a week, he started having more time for contemplation. As a result, he began getting painful insights into himself, as he got in touch with his feelings. He saw selfishness there. He often had done good deeds not out of a genuine expression of compassion for people's needs but as an attempt to gain the approval and praise of others, in order to compensate for feelings of inferiority. It took him three years to work through those reactions.

Was his decision worth it? Yes. He now experiences great peace and joy in his life. He enjoys intimate fellowship with his wife. He experiences mutual love with his children. He has learned to trust God—not himself—to rescue the world, while he still desires to play the part that God has for him. And he now accomplishes, through half the effort, many times more than he was accomplishing then, a feat he would have previously considered impossible.

His experience has been used in his own counseling ministry since that time, including with Reverend C, our case example. When Reverend C came for counseling, he was encouraged first to become informed about his obsessive-compulsive, perfectionist personality by reading the book, *The Workaholic and His Family.* Then he was helped to work through some of the conflicts his personality created.

Through counseling, he too came to realize that he needed to make priorities in his life and really find God's "light and easy yoke" for him. We encouraged him to work a forty- to fifty-hour work week and then spend the rest of his time with his family, in personal devotions, and seeing to other personal needs. He was encouraged to go ahead and say no to parishioners when he didn't have time to do certain things. When he did that, he felt guilt at first, and he had a few church members who became angry with him for not meeting all their needs or demands immediately. Having made the choice to put up with any such hostility, however, he was able to work through his own false guilt.

Reverend C discovered that, with more time to think and to feel, he also became more aware of his own depravity and selfish motives. He had to work through those and begin growing more toward Christlike maturity. He has done fine in his ministry since that time, has recovered from burnout, and now has the insights to prevent burnout from happening again.

Another suggestion by Dr. Congo is to "gain a clear sense of your purpose and priorities."[9] That is the apostle Paul's perspective on "reaping in due season." When a pastor drags in the front door at 11:00 P.M. following an unpleasant board meeting, only to discover urgent messages to return calls to three church members—two of whom are having major life crises and the third who is a major critic—it is difficult to maintain perspective. However, that is precisely the point at which he must focus on "due season."

Second, Paul maintained his perspective. Instead of focusing on the present, "what is seen" (2 Corinthians 4:18), his perspective was eternal; he focused on "what is unseen." Frequently, whether in vocational ministry or not, our focus is on the pressures, problems, conflicts, and frustrations that invariably will lead to burnout. Why didn't Paul burn out with all the adversities he experienced? His perspective enabled him to catalog his sufferings as "our light and momentary troubles are achieving for us an eternal glory that far outweighs them all" (v. 17). Such a perspective answers Dr. Congo's question, "Why, in a given church, does one pastor burn out and another thrive?" In summary, we can avoid burning out if we maintain perspective beyond present adversities.

Another important point to remember is that perspective is easier to maintain in relationship than in isolation. Dr. Herbert Freudenberger explains that when we experience burnout, we often seek detachment from support. He explains, "When you separate

9. Congo, p. 8.

yourself from people and events, you strip them of the power to hurt you. Unfortunately, you also diminish their power to affect you in positive ways."[10]

Based on what he wrote to the Galatians, if Paul were conducting a seminar or workshop on burnout today, he would not only underscore the importance of maintaining a perspective, he would urge those experiencing burnout, especially those in vocational ministry, to "carry one another's burdens." He might even point to his own example of keeping such men as Luke, Timothy, and Titus with him, or quote his call to Timothy to "get here before winter" (2 Timothy 4:21). To underscore the urgency of allowing time for peer support in ministry, Paul might add that the alternative is burnout.

In most churches, 80 percent of the work is done by 20 percent of the people. And, if the pastor feels that he himself is doing that 80 percent, then he needs to spread out the work, not just to one or two church members, who may then reach burnout themselves, but to many people. If the work doesn't get done, he should let the people see that. God will not have one hand tied behind His back and the world will not crash and disintegrate if we roll it and its burdens off our shoulders.

Finally, the temptation to quit always lurks just behind the next problem. The apostle Paul himself certainly experienced a multitude of pressures and faced the temptation to give up. However, in discussing the ministry he had received from God, he shared with his Corinthian readers the dynamic that enabled him to continue serving Christ despite adversity. As he explains in 2 Corinthians 4:16, "Therefore

10. Herbert Freudenberger and Geraldine Richelson, *Burn-Out* (New York: Anchor, Doubleday, 1980), p. 62.

we do not lose heart. Though outwardly we are wasting away, yet inwardly we are being renewed day by day." Despite being "hard pressed on every side, but not crushed; perplexed, but not in despair; persecuted, but not abandoned; struck down, but not destroyed," Paul did not give up. His outward man was "wasting away," but he was experiencing the inward renewal of the power of God's indwelling spirit. Paul had tapped into the source of inexhaustible spiritual power available to the inner man.

A minister's role is "to serve God," not to "burn out for God." Continued stress and burnout diminish a Christian worker's capacity to render effective service to others. Furthermore, for those in vocational ministry always to give out and not allow others to minister or give to them ignores the fundamental biblical truth that the body of Christ is to have different parts that minister to one another.

7

JESUS TREATS TWELVE TIRED MEN

During college days, one of our therapists suffered an arm injury during a basketball game. The arm was X-rayed by an orthopedic surgeon, who said no bones had been broken. After a few days' rest, the student resumed his basketball activities, as well as a job that involved lifting heavy boxes.

When, over a period of weeks, pain in the arm persisted and then worsened, the student returned to the orthopedist. A new set of X-rays showed the wrist now had a complete break. The arm had to be immobilized, and the stress of lifting boxes and playing basketball had to stop.

So it is with burnout. As seen in previous chapters, the stresses of life can lead to physical, emotional, and spiritual symptoms of burnout. Then, when these symptoms persist, it is imperative that stress levels be lightened so that recovery can begin.

Jesus recognized that when He saw His disciples return from a missionary trip on which He had sent them. In Mark 6:7, Jesus' great Galilean ministry is drawing to a close. Multitudes had thronged to hear His words and witness His miracles. The stress of those busy days for Jesus and His followers was compounded by a rising opposition on the part of the Pharisees, the official religious leaders of Israel. During that time, our Savior was particularly gripped with feelings of compassion toward the multitudes, whom He characterized as "harassed and helpless, like sheep without a shepherd" (Matthew 9:36).

At that point, Christ implemented a new phase of His ministry. It is described in Mark 6: "Calling the Twelve to him, he sent them out two by two. . . . They went out and preached that people should repent. They drove out many demons and anointed many sick people with oil and healed them. . . . The apostles gathered around Jesus and reported to him all they had done and taught" (vv. 7, 12-13, 30).

Mark interrupted the telling of the disciples' mission to explain to his readers of the death of John the Baptist (vv. 14-29), which evidently came about the time the twelve had set out on their mission. It's not difficult to sense just how stressful that time must have been for the twelve.

Several factors indicate how their stress may have risen to burnout levels. First, Mark's use of the word *apostles* in verse 30, coupled with the description of Christ's giving them authority (v. 7), indicates that that was their first official mission on their own. They were like novice salesmen who had completed their training and just set out with their materials into their assigned territory, or like a college quarterback who suddenly finds himself, after many practices, at the helm of the offensive team during the first regular-season game.

Coupled with the pressure to do well was the reality of spiritual opposition—"and gave them authority over evil spirits" (v. 7); the necessity of trusting God for providing their day-to-day needs—"Take nothing for the journey except a staff—no bread, no bag, no money in your belts. Wear sandals but not an extra tunic" (vv. 8-9); the constant drain of living out of a suitcase—"Whenever you enter a house, stay there until you leave that town" (v. 10); and the ever-present threat of personal rejection—"And if any place will not welcome you or listen to you, shake the dust off your feet when you leave, as a testimony against them" (v. 11). Then, after busy months of ministry and travel, they returned to Jesus and were informed of the tragic death of John the Baptist. By that time, they were prime candidates for burnout.

Although Mark's account of their debriefing (v. 30) indicates that Christ wanted to hear their report, it also indicates that He was more concerned about the effects their mission had on them than He was about hearing what they had done. None of the gospels record that any of Christ's comments were critical of their ministry. However, Mark indicated that Christ's immediate concern was to relieve their pressure.

That incident highlights an important principle for employers, supervisors, and Christian leaders. It is often easy to become so concerned with "getting the job done" or "doing it right" that we lose sight of the needs of the people who are actually carrying on the work. That is especially true if the employer or supervisor is an obsessive-compulsive workaholic too. Our Savior displayed a type of personal concern and compassion needed today when He said to His disciples, "Come with me by yourselves to a quiet place and get some rest [or 'rest a while,' KJV]" (Mark 6:31). He sensed that the burnout factor was present in them, so, although there was a vast number of people still unreached, He instructed them to take a break.

A close examination of Christ's brief statement shows there are three key elements that, when combined, can relieve the stresses that lead to burnout. These are (1) a change in location, (2) a change in activity or responsibility, and (3) a certain amount of time.

A CHANGE IN LOCATION

It is significant that Christ did not simply say, "Take a break." He specifically told His disciples to come aside, or change location, to a quiet place. In fact, the term Christ uses for the location to which the disciples were directed suggests that it was a remote or solitary place. Christ knew His disciples would be unable to experience relief from stress as long as they were in contact with "so many people . . . coming and going that they did not even have a chance to eat" (v. 31).

Regular vacations with a change of locale and even occasional "getaways" or "mini-vacations" are an important part of preventing burnout or of relieving burnout once it has occurred.

How does a psychiatrist escape burnout? One has developed a mountain retreat in a neighboring state to which he makes regular visits. For him, that change in location from a busy urban ministry to the quiet solitude of mountain greenery is an important key to preventing burnout.

Whether your getaway place is a nearby campground, the mountains, the beach, or just a weekend "escape package" at a nearby hotel, it is important to carve out time for a change of scenery.

A CHANGE IN ACTIVITY

The second factor seen in Christ's instructions is a change in activity or responsibility. It is significant that the same person who sent them on their ministry mission now tells them to rest up. The particular word used by Christ, which can be accurately trans-

lated "rest up," indicates that the disciples themselves needed to take the initiative to do that. So it is
with an individual experiencing stress today. Often, a
person may know he or she should rest, but there is a
temptation not to take time to do so. Eventually, the
discovery is made that failure to get proper rest is a
shortcut to burnout.

For years, a minister in a busy pastorate also
carried an early morning radio ministry. Late night
board and committee meetings, as well as ministry
phone calls, were followed by the sound of a 4:00 A.M.
alarm clock to prepare for radio ministry that began
at six. When years of that frantic schedule began to
take its toll, the concerned advice of friends was
heeded. The radio ministry and schedule were modi-
fied and burnout was averted.

A CHANGE FOR A TIME

The third element in Christ's instructions to his
disciples is an amount of time. The tense of the verb
"to rest" indicates a relatively short period of time.
The point is that a planned amount of time should be
taken for a change in location and activity. That was
particularly needed in light of the description of their
surroundings during the debriefing—crowds of people meeting each other coming and going, leaving the
disciples with no spare moment to call their own,
even in order to eat.

That description of the disciples' circumstances
may strike a responsive chord with you. If so, perhaps Jesus is also telling you, "Come with me by
yourselves to a quiet place and get some rest."

A final glance at the disciples in this chapter
surfaces two important facts. First, they did take action to alleviate the stresses that lead to burnout. "So

they went away by themselves in a boat to a solitary place" (v. 32). However, when they reached that solitary place, there were already crowds there waiting for them, so their getaway didn't last long. Nevertheless, the boat journey itself was at least a short time of change of location and activity away from the crowds.

The continued demands of people for ministry, however, ultimately contributed to the dulling of their spiritual perception. When they saw Jesus feed the five thousand in that solitary place, with only five loaves of bread and two fish, they were still too numb to take it all in. As a result, when they saw Jesus walking on the water later that night, "they were completely amazed, for they had not understood about the loaves; their hearts were hardened" (vv. 51-52). Burnout can leave one so hardened or disillusioned with the world that one has little emotional or spiritual energy left to comprehend the supernatural or the meaning behind it.

The lesson to be learned from these twelve tired men is evident. When the stresses of life are building to the burnout level, it is time to consider a change of location, a change in activity or responsibility, and an amount of time in which to take a break. The alternative may be burnout.

8

STARTING THE UPWARD
SPIRAL PHYSICALLY

Escaping or reversing burnout primarily involves taking care of yourself physically, mentally, and spiritually, allowing God and others to help you in that task. But, first of all, you have to decide to take the initiative yourself, realizing that taking care of self is a responsibility given us by God. Without meeting that responsibility, we will never be able to succeed in the life-long purposes He has for us.

TAKING CARE OF YOURSELF

At our clinic, we have patients complete a "Taking Care of Yourself" test, which gives them and us some idea of how well they are accomplishing that God-given task. We have divided these test questions into three categories: the physical, emotional, and spiritual, even though some of the questions include elements of more than one category.

The following are the questions to the physical parts of this questionnaire and the advice we give our patients, including those suffering from burnout. Except in cases of suicidal thinking (discussed in the next chapter), we advocate making changes in the physical areas of a burnout victim's life first. Just feeling better physically often begins to change a person's burned out emotions and gives them the strength to begin other changes—physical, emotional, and spiritual.

PHYSICAL CARE

1. Did you exercise three times this past week?
The medical profession has maintained for years that being in good physical condition makes a noticeable difference in longevity, and good health. Exercise can help keep off weight, keep blood pressure under control, keep the heart healthy, and even ward off other diseases.

We have known that individuals become addicted to negative things, such as drugs and alcohol. However, we now know that they can become addicted to positive things also. William Glasser showed that people can become addicted to jogging. Such an addiction has a physical reason. Certain chemicals are released from the body during jogging and other healthful exercise that cause a sense of well being.

Scripture also indicates that physical training is of some value (1 Timothy 4:8). Being in good physical shape will aid your effectiveness for Christ.

2. Did you eat a balanced diet this week?
Diet is a major factor in the realm of physical health. Most nutritionists agree that the best diet is a balanced one that includes a little of all the food groups—meat and other proteins, vegetables, fruit, dairy products, and bread, cereals, and other grain products.

If you need to be on a weight-reducing diet, make sure it includes all the food groups, but less of each. The only way to lose weight and keep it off, healthily, is to reduce your calories and to exercise more. An important tip to remember is to ask yourself as you start to eat something, "Am I eating this to please God or to please myself?" Another important factor is not to base your self-worth on your physical appearance but on your position—who you are in Christ.

3. Did you get eight hours of sleep per night most nights this week?

Many people boast that they can get by on little sleep, but studies show that most adults need about eight hours of sleep per night to function at their best and to stay healthy. Children need even more. For example, an elementary school child may need ten or eleven hours, a junior high school student nine or ten, and a high school student eight to nine. Some elderly people, however, can get by on less than eight hours.

When we don't have enough sleep, we tend to be irritable, more critical, more depressed, have a harder time concentrating, work less efficiently, and enjoy life less. Actually, we can't serve God well if we aren't getting proper rest. Sleep is essential to sound mental, emotional, and spiritual health.

God Himself set a good example for us when He rested after creating the world over a six-day period. "On the seventh day he rested from all his work" (Genesis 2:2).

4. How much of a "Type A" personality are you?

The medical profession defines a "Type A" personality as one who is time oriented and never seems to have enough time. He tends to be competitive and success-oriented, a workaholic, often doing two or more things at once. That type of personality may experience a great deal of underlying anger behind the success orientation and have a stronger need to produce in order to feel succesful. Such persons are prone to heart disease and, statistically, are more likely to die young.

It is important for the Type A personality to slow down, relax, and put priorities in proper order. Type A personalities tend to move, walk, and eat rapidly. They also tend to hurry those with whom they are talking. Type A's get upset when waiting (in traffic or when placed on hold in a telephone conversation) and when they must perform repetitive tasks. They try to schedule things tighter and tighter in order to get more things done. Even taking a short break from work or taking time to relax and do nothing produces guilt.

Since Type A persons usually live life on a schedule—a tight schedule—they must rearrange that schedule to include time to relax, time with the Lord, time with children and mate, time just to goof off, and after all that, then their scheduled time for work. For most people, of course, that will involve the normal forty-hour work week, and when absolutely necessary, up to fifty hours—but no more. Then, after rearranging their schedule according to priorities, they must determine to follow it.

If you are a Type A, you need to develop an ability to slow down. To do that, become aware of your need to take life slower. Take deep, slow breaths to aid in the slowing down process. Review your former priorities and be determined to be content with completing or accomplishing perhaps half as many tasks a day as you would normally try to do, remembering that taking care of yourself and the emotional and spiritual needs of your loved ones is your first priority. For some, that means getting away for a while, for others, it means saying no to heading up that committee yet another year. Each of us is responsible for finding ways to be responsible toward himself.

LEARN TIME MANAGEMENT SKILLS

To spend less pressured time with work, time management skills may need to be sharpened. Will Rogers once said, "It's not so much what you do each day, it's what gets done that counts." Although this is not a book on time management, some practical suggestions are in order.

1. *Take inventory of your usage of time.* Invest time in scheduling, making lists of things to be accomplished, and prioritizing that list. Plan ahead, allowing sufficient time for interruptions. Beware of "time bandits," those things that intrude into your schedule and rob you of precious minutes and hours that could be used to accomplish the task at hand.

2. *Learn to concentrate on the task at hand.* Work at screening out distractions. Learn to distinguish between essential details and nonessentials.

3. *Be able to grasp the big picture.* Work at "majoring on the majors." Be sure to relate your daily tasks to overall life goals and even to "five-year goals."

4. *Work at being decisive.* Get all the information available and then make a decision. Don't put it off. Avoid procrastination.

5. *Learn to delegate, particularly those things that can be done effectively by other people.* Don't spread yourself too thin. Concentrate your time and energies on doing those few things you are best at doing.

Making changes in all these physical areas of your life will take time. However, as you start them, you will begin to find the physical strength to start making changes emotionally and spiritually as well.

9
STARTING THE UPWARD SPIRAL EMOTIONALLY

Before addressing those things that you can do to take care of yourself emotionally, we must address an emotional problem of the most severe burnout victim, that of suicidal thinking.

REVERSING SUICIDAL THINKING

A woman phoned in to our radio talk show recently to tell about her daughter who had been burned out and depressed. The depression had become a major one. She had voiced suicidal thoughts to her family on several occasions, but, partly because she was a Christian, they had not taken her seriously. Eventually, the daughter killed herself. The woman who phoned in did so to warn listeners to take seriously the suicidal thoughts of loved ones.

Anyone who is talking about suicide or who admits to having suicidal thoughts should be under professional care, preferably by a Christian psychiatrist or psychologist. Anyone who has a "suicide plan" should be hospitalized immediately.

To the severely depressed who have lost hope, suicide may seem the only way out of their situation. A severely burned out and depressed Christian may even become convinced that it is God's will, that God no longer wants him or her in this world. The Bible, however, shows that suicide is a sin equivalent to murder. The Scriptures record seven suicides: Abimelech (Judges 9:54), Samson (Judges 16:30), Saul (1 Samuel 31:43), Saul's armor bearer (1 Samuel 31:5), Ahithophel (2 Samuel 17:23), Zimri (1 Kings 16:18), and Judas Iscariot (Matthew 27:3-5). It is clear that none of those were in the will of God.

A common misconception involves the fear that to mention suicide to a depressed person will bring about thoughts that have not occurred previously or will increase the likelihood of a suicide attempt. Actually, to lovingly confront a person with a question about suicidal thoughts can be the first step toward reversing suicidal thinking, as it was with the depressed salesman, Mr. I, our case example whose pastor questioned him. Mr. I then spent four weeks in the hospital under our care. He was able to reverse his burnout and depression and to put his marriage and life back together.

In our ministry, we have developed ten warning signs of individuals who are most likely to attempt suicide. Several of these, as you will notice, have a close relationship with burnout.

WARNING SIGNS OF SUICIDE

1. Intense emotional pain, as seen in severe depression
2. Intense feelings of hopelessness
3. A prior history of a suicide attempt, or voiced warnings of suicidal intentions
4. Severe health problems
5. A significant loss—death of a spouse, loss of a job, and so on
6. Forming of a suicide plan
7. Chronic self-destructive behavior—alcoholism, an eating disorder, and so on
8. An intense need to achieve

9. An excess of disturbing life events within the past six months
10. Someone who is single, male, white, and more than forty-five years of age, who has experienced some of the above signs

TAKING CARE OF SELF—EMOTIONALLY

If your burnout has not reached the severe stage of suicidal thinking, our "Taking Care of Yourself" test includes a number of steps you can take personally to help reverse the emotional part of your burnout.

1. Have you laughed several times today?
A wise man once compared a cheerful or merry heart to good medicine (Proverbs 17:22). Laughter is a sign of good mental health. Medical studies indicate that laughter releases chemicals called endorphins in the brain, promoting feelings of well being. Author Norman Cousins helped himself recover from a debilitating disease by watching old film comedies and cartoons, allowing himself to laugh every day as part of his healing process. the absence of frequent laughter may be an external symptom indicating the presence of deeper emotional conflicts.

2. What percentage of your self-talk was positive today?
Each of us talks to ourselves. The way in which we talk to ourselves has a great deal to do with how we feel. Self-talk that is negative, derogatory, or critical fosters depression. Make an effort to be more positive, kind, and forgiving in the things you say to yourself. Why not set aside a time to consider how you talk to yourself? Look for specific changes. For-

give yourself when necessary and move on from personal failures.

3. What amount of time this past week did you spend living in the present?

Many people focus on past failures or past accomplishments. Either focus can be damaging to good mental health. Often when we are depressed, we focus on the past. It is important that we live in the here and now.

Another misplaced focus is dwelling only on what may happen in the future. Jesus says in Matthew 6:34, "Therefore do not worry about tomorrow, for tomorrow will worry about itself. Each day has enough trouble of its own." Anxiety causes that misplaced focus on the possible problems of tomorrow. Because of God's sovereign control, however, tomorrow will take care of itself.

Learn to deal with your past, look forward to your future, and live properly one day at a time in the here and now.

4. Did you do something three times this week for relaxation and recreation?

Maintaining good mental health often involves learning to relax. It is worthwhile to plan, at least three times a week, activities specifically dedicated to enjoyable recreation, something not connected with your usual line of work. If you are experiencing burnout or near burnout, try some recreational and relaxing activities other than your usual, since they obviously are not helping your situation.

That is particularly true of the one who views a lot of television, trying to forget the worries of the day through watching the traumas of make-believe characters. Watching make-believe, or even someone else's real life, is never a substitute for experiencing life yourself. Instead, shoot some baskets with your kids or play some table games with the whole family. Do those activities for fun, without a highly competitive attitude. Occasionally, you might even play less than your best in order to let the other person win. It will be good for his or her self-esteem and sense of pleasure, and for your sense of values.

If a job or vocation is exceedingly stressful, tiring, frustrating, or boring over a long period of time, perhaps a change in responsibilities, activities, job, or career needs to be considered. If possible, a sabbatical may be in order. But make sure the change is to positive types of activities, although less demanding ones. Don't act on a burnout impulse to become a full-time hermit, beach bum, or occasional tinkerer.

For two of our case examples, consideration of changing jobs brought different decisions.

The eighteen-year-old factory worker, Mr. F, did go back to his job temporarily. Meanwhile, he received vocational testing at our clinic and found that he had gifts in some other areas. Also, he discovered that his type of personality would not tolerate a monotonous job. (Some people can do monotonous work and even seem to thrive on it. They block out the monotony and just seem to enjoy themselves. Other people need new and different challenges.)

Eventually, Mr. F quit his job and began work as a carpenter, where he could do different things each day and see the work of his hands begin to make a house take shape. Only when he changed jobs to one more compatible with his personality did he recover completely from his burnout.

Mrs. E, the mental health worker who counseled depressed people, was encouraged to take a different tack. To continue working in such a specific and difficult area, she found that thirty hours of counseling a week, instead of her former fifty to sixty hours, was all that she could handle effectively. She was then able to spend more time relaxing and working in her church. A change of pace and rearrangement of her schedule, rather than a change of job, was the key to reversing her burnout.

LEARN STRESS MANAGEMENT

Although a certain amount of stress is necessary and even good, our response to stress can make us capable of meeting more of the necessary stresses of life successfully. And although a lifting of as much stress as possible may be necessary to recover from current burnout, stress management needs to be learned to avoid future burnout. That involves:

- learning when it is appropriate to say no, both to yourself and to others who may place demands on you
- learning when it is appropriate to settle for limited objectives
- being able to distinguish between situations in which you should respond with your "flight or fight" defense mechanism in gear and those in which you should take a less concerned approach

We must learn to recognize our limitations as human and, when we sense that we are close to our limit, take a deep breath, relax, and seek—at least temporarily—a change of pace, a change of place, and a change of perspective. If you think you can't afford a vacation, then make it a financial priority and plan and budget for it.

   5. How often were you stuck on "Plan A" this month?
   "Plan A" is your routine schedule. It includes all

the things you normally do each day from the time you get up to the time you go to bed. Plan A includes the events of your day, your activities, your habits, and your appearance. People often become depressed because they are following Plan A.

If your Plan A is leading to frequent bouts with burnout and depression, it may be time to form a Plan B. That may involve coming up with five to ten specific things you can do in a given period of time, say a week, to change how you feel. Recreational activities mentioned above would be a part of that. Other changes to your plan may include just rearranging your before-work activities. If you feel sluggish until you eat breakfast, eat breakfast when you first get up. If you have trouble keeping your eyes open when reading your Bible first thing in the morning, take a shower first. If finding something to wear each morning is a great frustration, start laying out clothes the night before.

When developing Plan B, set aside specific time to invest in time with the Lord. Include one meaningful social contact each day, by phone if necessary. Develop a daily routine that includes some variety and is more personally satisfying, if only in the little things. People who are more emotionally oriented tend to become bored more quickly. Variety in daily life helps that.

Plan B should also include refreshing Sundays or whatever day you have off. Scripture says the "Sabbath" should include refreshment, no work, celebration of our relationship with God, assembling together with Christian friends and with relatives, and enjoying life.*

---

*Note: although the New Testament doesn't mention the Mosaic command to observe the Sabbath, the Sabbath-rest principle existed in the Mosaic law.

6. How much change have you experienced during the past year?

Because of the mobile society in which we live, change is a major factor in life. Changes in residence, employment, or schools all produce stress points. Medical studies show that if too many stress points accumulate during any one year, there is a great likelihood of developing significant physical or emotional problems. The Holmes-Rahe Stress Test was designed to identify the number and severity of stress factors experienced by an individual during the preceding year. A total of two hundred or more stress points can indicate the presence of or likelihood of burnout.

THE STRESS OF ADJUSTING TO CHANGES[1]

Events	Scale of Impact
Death of a spouse	100
Divorce	73
Marital separation	65
Jail term	63
Death of close family member	63
Personal injury or illness	53
Marriage	50
Fired at work	47
Marital reconciliation	45
Retirement	45
Change in health of family member	44
Pregnancy	40
Sex difficulties	39
Gain of new family member	39

1. Reprinted with permission of T. H. Holmes and R. H. Rahe, "The Social Adjustment Rating Scale," *Journal of Psychosomatic Research,* II:213. Copyright 1967, Pergamon Press.

Business readjustment	39
Change in financial state	38
Death of close friend	37
Change to different line of work	36
Change in number of arguments with spouse	35
Mortgage over $10,000	31
Foreclosure of mortgage or loan	30
Change in responsibilities at work	29
Son or daughter leaving home	29
Trouble with in-laws	29
Outstanding personal achievement	28
Wife begins or stops work	26
Begin or end school	26
Change in living conditions	25
Revision of personal habits	24
Trouble with boss	23
Change in work hours or conditions	20
Change in residence	20
Change in schools	19
Change in recreation	19
Change in church activities	19
Change in social activities	18
Mortgage or loan less than $10,000	17
Change in sleeping habits	16
Change in number of family get-togethers	15
Change in eating habits	15
Vacation	13
Christmas	12
Minor violations of the law	11

7. Is the sexual part of your life healthy?

Proper sexual function plays a role in preventing burnout. For married people, that involves application of the principle explained by Solomon in Proverbs 5:15-21. In that section, Solomon established two important principles regulating our sexual nature.

Principle 1: Since God created us male and female, it is both normal and desirable for husbands and wives to enjoy the romance and excitement of marital love.

That principle is consistent with what Paul explains in 1 Corinthians 7:1-5. It is also talked about by Solomon in the following verses. Note the vivid word pictures used by Solomon to capture the essence of marital romance:

> Drink water from your own cistern,
>   running water from your own well.
> Should your spring overflow in the streets,
>   your streams of water in the public squares?
> Let them be yours alone,
>   never to be shared with strangers.
> May your fountain be blessed,
>   and may you rejoice in the wife of your youth.
> A loving doe, a graceful deer—
>   may her breasts satisfy you always,
>   may you ever be captivated by her love.
>   (Proverbs 5:15-19)

Principle 2: Sexual misconduct displeases God and will produce serious consequences.

For the married person that means remaining true to one's mate not only physically but in thought, word, and deed.

For the single person, that involves a discipline and commitment to purity consistent with 1 Corinthians 6:19-20. Public opinion seems to indicate that a majority of adults—61 percent, including 78 percent of young adults, according to a recent Roper Organization survey—now believe that premarital sex is not morally wrong. That, however, does not change the negative feelings premarital sex produces. These include feelings of unease, frustration, and guilt—real guilt—which involves holding back, a less than complete and unending commitment to the present and future well-being of the other person. As Dick Purnell says in his book *Becoming a Friend and Lover,* in the marriage relationship,

> there is safety and security. . . without fear of abandonment. There is also total freedom from guilt in sex. You can know that God smiles on and is pleased with your sexual relationship. . . . Outside of marriage, guilt eats away at the individuals until the relationship is either destroyed or crippled. . . . Stimulated by lifetime commitment and the absence of guilt . . . we are able to be ourselves totally and to be emotionally "naked" without fear. . . . When we have sex outside the boundaries that God has set up for our protection and provision, we end up cheating ourselves.[2]

Such feelings of unease, frustration, and guilt produce added stress in a single person's life instead of relieving it. The added stress of a sexual relationship lacking lifetime commitment adds to those factors that can create burnout and make it harder to recover from burnout. God's laws regarding sex are meant as a protection (physically, emotionally, and spiritually), not as a limitation to our pleasure and fulfillment.

In Proverbs 5, observe the graphic way in which Solomon describes the consequences of sexual misconduct.

> Why be captivated, my son, by an adulteress?
>   Why embrace the bosom of another man's wife?
> For a man's ways are in full view of the Lord,
>   and he examines all his paths.

2. Dick Purnell, *Becoming a Friend and Lover* (San Bernardino, Calif.: Here's Life, 1986), pp. 58-59.

The evil deeds of a wicked man ensnare him;
   the cords of his sin hold him fast.
He will die for lack of discipline,
   led astray by his own great folly.
                              (Proverbs 5:20-23)

For singles, maintaining sexual purity and learning how to relate to others in close friendships before marriage alleviates stress and burnout, as Purnell's *Becoming a Friend and Lover* so aptly shows. For married couples, maintaining marital romance, and cultivating the sparkle of an intimate relationship can add zest to life and help prevent burnout. For help in that regard, see the book, *Sex in the Christian Marriage.*[3]

8. Have you done something good—physically, psychologically, or spiritually—for one person this week?

The age in which we are living is a self-involved, "me" generation. The selfish spirit of this age can be mentally unhealthy. The apostle Paul expresses his concern for an "others orientation" in Philippians 2:4: "Each of you should look not only to your own interests, but also to the interests of others." Physically, you might help someone with chores or errands. Psychologically, you might provide someone with counsel or just a listening ear. Spiritually, you might share what the Lord has been teaching you. We are emotionally enriched when we invest ourselves in others. Christ reminds us in Luke 6:38 that giving comes back to us in like measure and more.

3. Richard Meier et al., *Sex in the Christian Marriage* (Richardson, Tex.: Today Publishers, 1985). Distributed by Baker Book House, Grand Rapids.

9. Have you forgiven the last three people who offended you?

Forgiveness is important because, if we don't forgive others, we tend to turn our anger inward, which results in bitterness and then in depression. Forgiveness involves, by an act of the will, choosing to no longer hold a grudge against an offending party. It is inaccurate to say, "I cannot forgive," since forgiveness is a matter of the will. We can say, "I will forgive with God's help." The measure of forgiving each other is "just as in Christ God forgave you" (Ephesians 4:32). It is important when we were offended to quickly choose to forgive rather than to harbor grudges.

10. How many times has envy affected you this year?

Allowing envy towards others to continue leads to depression. Solomon said, "A heart at peace gives life to the body, but envy rots the bones" (Proverbs 14:30). Solomon recognized the effect of positive or negative emotions on our physical being. A proper response to the success of others is to be happy for them. Solomon says in Ecclesiastes that when we desire to prove that we are more important than others, which is the basis for envy, we are like a person chasing the wind, which is futile. It is important to be grateful for what we have received from the Lord. When envy surfaces, remember that none of us deserves anything. Whatever we get from life is a gift from the Lord.

11. Did you talk with your spouse (or, if single, a close friend or relative) three times this week about your feelings?

Emotional problems often come when we have

repressed our feelings instead of dealing with them. It is important to sit down with our spouse (or roommate or close friend) and share both the good and bad events of the day. Sharing feelings also is important when resolving areas of marital conflict. Men generally tend to hide their feelings more than women and may need to work specifically at that.

Tips for conflict resolution include:

- Use "I" messages—"I feel," "I need," "I want"—instead of "you" statements—"you should," "you shouldn't."
- Avoid attacking each other's character; explain only the specific behavior that offends.
- Ask for some kind of specific change, keep the issues to the present, and avoid bringing up the past.
- Listen to your spouse.
- Don't let your emotions get out of hand.
- Resist the temptation to keep track of who won past conflicts. Recognize that when someone wins a marital conflict, everyone loses.
- Ask for and give feedback to each other.
- Schedule time to discuss feelings with your mate.

12. Did you share your burdens with a friend this week?

A successful, intelligent, hard-working businessman suffered a major heart attack. During his recovery he become close friends with one of us. During a telephone conversation, he remarked, "You are about the only person I feel I can really call a close friend." What is remarkable about his statement is that his experience typifies that of many candidates for burnout.

Most people who experience depression or burnout do not have even one friend to whom they are close enough to share their personal feelings and still feel loved and accepted. An important step in maintaining an emotional balance is to develop close friendships. Each of us needs about six people with whom we can share our true feelings and still feel loved. It is hard for any person, even a mate, to have the full burden of all our feelings, particularly if he or she is going through an emotionally heavy period, too.

Of course, if you are already in burnout, building a friendship may be hard to do, although if someone offers friendship and unconditional understanding at this time, don't rebuff it. It's what you need, even if you have little emotional energy to offer them anything in return. Allow others to give friendship to you. After you recover from burnout, the give and take of friendships will be important to keeping your life balanced.

If you still have the emotional energy, start looking for friends, ones who will be good listeners, who will be loyal, and who will care, but also who will be willing to give a viewpoint different from yours if they feel it is needed. The book of Proverbs has a great deal to say about friendship, including the reminder that "a friend loves at all times" (Proverbs 17:17), and "wounds from a friend can be trusted, but an enemy multiplies kisses" (Proverbs 27:6). Find someone with whom you can relate, then spend time with that person developing a growing friendship and building mutual trust.

Beginning a relationship may involve challenging another person to become involved in helping balance each other's lives. If you both need to reduce your weight, you might agree to call each other every evening to list what you have eaten that day. If you need to spend more time in the Word or in quality time with family members, work out a similar reporting arrangement with someone from your workplace, church, or neighborhood. Such a reporting system may get you active in making personal changes, be a helping hand to someone else, and help build a casual relationship toward becoming a closer friendship, all at the same time.

13. Did you do at least one specific thing this week to become closer to a relative—a parent, brother, sister, or other close relative?

Each of us has a family heritage, one that has tremendous bearing on our mental health. Often a need exists to go back and mend or repair relationships, building a new way of relating that can lead to good mental and emotional stability. It is important to take the initiative to build a closer relationship with your family, rather than waiting on others in the family to take the lead. Doing at least one thing per week—perhaps a phone call, a letter, a visit, or an outing—with extended family members can build closer relationships and foster emotional health.

ACTIONS LEAD TO EMOTIONS

If you see a lot of areas above that need changing in your life, you may think, "But I just don't feel like doing all that!" particularly if you are already feeling the effects of burnout. However, an important principle to improving one's life is that proper actions lead to proper emotions. We frequently find that true in our counseling. The most dramatic illustration of that, perhaps, is in marital counseling. Often, a husband or wife will say, "I just don't feel like trying any more. I've lost that feeling of love for my mate." In such cases, our counsel is to act like you love your spouse and, pretty soon, you will begin to feel like you love your mate as well. Many initially respond with unbelief to that statement but come back later saying in joyous astonishment that it works.

The same approach can work in your own relationship with God, with others, and with yourself. Begin taking some of those needed steps to revitalize your life, to begin to reverse that burnout spiral, whether you feel like doing them or not. The actions of doing the right thing will soon be followed by the desire to do them, and you'll be on the upward spiral, moving away from the depths of burnout.

10
STARTING THE UPWARD SPIRAL SPIRITUALLY

The spiritual part of burnout victims' lives has been neglected, although sometimes they don't realize it. Some burnout victims do realize it but believe that their special situation made it completely impossible to keep up an adequate spiritual life. Usually, changing one's priorities and even canceling out activities that were previously thought to be important priorities, as mentioned in the previous chapter, are necessary to finding the time to recuperate from burnout spiritually.

If you doubt that the quality of your spiritual life has had any effect on your burnout, see how many of the following questions from our "Taking Care of Yourself" test you can answer positively.

1. Does the Word of God still give you a thrill?
Although emotions are not always an accurate guide for gauging response to the Scriptures, the nature of the Word of God indicates that it should give us an emotional lift. Meditating on the Word of God allows God to speak to us personally through the words that apply, in one way or another, to all of us. Do you look at God's Word as His love letter to you?

One danger faced by many Christians, especially those in vocational ministries, may be over-familiarity with and a loss of wonder at God's Word, produced by the constant handling of Scriptures. We should work at developing an attitude of awe toward the Scriptures. The book of Psalms begins, "Blessed is the man . . . [whose] delight is in the law of the Lord; and on his law he meditates day and night. He is like a tree planted by streams of water, which yields its fruit in season and whose leaf does not wither."

A number of factors may be involved in causing us to lose that thrill over the Scriptures: depression, sin in our lives, a habit of neglecting to spend time with God in the Word, approaching the Scriptures only from an academic or teacher's viewpoint, or never having been genuinely saved.

If you have not trusted Jesus Christ as your personal Savior and Lord, acknowledge that to do so is not only the key to overcoming burnout but also the ultimate answer to meaning and purpose in life.

Acknowledge to God that you are a sinner (that you have not and cannot, on your own, live up to His desires for your life), and that you yourself cannot bridge the gap that your sins have caused between you and God. Realize that Christ's death was the punishment you deserve for your sins. Having taken your punishment upon Himself, His death and resurrection became the basis for the forgiveness of your sins and for your coming into a close and completed relationship with God. Depend on His death and resurrection to cancel your debt to God.

Then trust Him as your personal Savior from a life, here and eternally, without God. Realize that His Holy Spirit then resides in your life to lead you, comfort you, empower you, and to allow you to feel God's love for you.

It is worth the effort to work to recapture joy in personally communicating with God through Bible reading and study.

2. Do you enjoy the old hymns of the faith?

In addition to reflecting on our relationship with God through the Bible, the old hymns of our faith can produce good psychological and mental health. The composers of those hymns wrote them, not because they had a job to do, but because the thoughts and concepts about God they express thrilled them so much that they were compelled to share their spiritual joy with others in that manner. The next time you sing a hymn or just read the words of one, think of the joy and devotion to God that those words produced in the composer.

The older hymns, generally, are characterized by simple but profound messages; by easy memorization, because they contain a great deal of repetition; and by drawing biblical truth together with human experience, which can produce a satisfying spiritual and emotional response. Try singing a hymn to God as you begin and as you finish your daily devotions. You might even keep a hymnbook with your Bible for such a purpose.

3. Did you apply the Word of God to your life daily this past week?

Contrary to the opinion of some specialists in both fields, the Bible and psychiatry are not incompatible, as long as the Bible is the final authority. Scripture memorization can be a useful tool for maintaining good mental health. As Solomon exhorted, regarding God-given instructions: "My son, pay attention to what I say; listen closely to my words. Do not let them out of your sight, keep them within your heart; for they are life to those who find them and health to a man's whole body" (Proverbs 4:20-22).

God promised Joshua prosperity and success through meditating on and applying God's Word.

Be careful to obey all the law . . .do not turn from it to the right or to the left, that you may be succesful wherever you go. Do not let this Book of the Law depart from your mouth; meditate on it day and night, so that you may be careful to do everything written in it. Then you will be prosperous and successful. . . . Do not be discouraged, for the Lord your God will be with you wherever you go." (Joshua 1:7-9)

Set a goal of memorizing three verses a week to bring your perspective back into focus, and then consciously apply those verses to your life over several days' time. Don't start out, however, as many Type A's might, trying to memorize too many verses a week, giving little time to really meditate and apply each verse memorized. Also, setting too high a goal, if not met, can cause false or unnecessary guilt and even cause you to give up on the whole process.

Memorized verses can help keep you from sin, especially when, because of tiredness, you are more prone to temptation. Memorized words popping back into your mind become a special hedge against temptation.

Also, as you study the Bible each morning, over and beyond the verses you memorize, look for one or two special concepts and commands that you can apply to your life that day.

4. How often this past month has Proverbs 8:36, "He who sins against me injures himself" (NASB*) applied to you?

Many individuals, including Christians, fail to understand the reasons for God's laws. They think they were set up only to test our blind and unquestioning obedience to God—that His primary desire is

*New American Standard Bible.

for complete dictatorship, and so He sits in heaven with a big stick, just waiting for us to get out of line. That there are loving, caring, and reasonable bases behind His laws and that they were set up for our best interests does not occur to them. God knows that if we live in light of His principles, life will be more enjoyable and meaningful. When we sin against God, we are indeed hurting ourselves. When we disobey God, our self-concept is lowered and we experience a lower sense of self-worth. By claiming God's power through His Holy Spirit, we can resist temptation and yield to God.

5. When needed, how quickly do you apply 1 John 1:9 to your life?
"If we confess our sins, he is faithful and just and will forgive us our sins and purify us from all unrighteousness."

When we do sin, God's forgiveness is always sufficient and immediately available. Although some Christians tend to ignore sin in their lives, others have a hard time applying the principle of 1 John 1:9 because of a desire to punish themselves. "Confess" doesn't mean saying, "I'm sorry." It means "to agree with God" that what we have done is wrong. It also requires a desire to change that behavior. We need to determine that by His grace we will confess—agree with His assessment of what we've done—and then accept His forgiveness, forgive ourselves, seek to make needed changes, and, finally, forget the situation and move on.

God is a just God, but He also is a loving Father. He waits with outstretched arms for us to come back to Him and agree with Him that our sin, which severed our fellowship or companionship with Him, was wrong. It is important to remember that Christ has paid for our sins already, in full. Consequently, it is not our place to try to punish ourselves or pay for our own sins. Also, because Christ has already paid for our sins, we never lose our salvation, no matter how much we sin. We accepted salvation as a free gift, neither earned or deserved. Although fellowship or companionship with God can be broken, confession of sin restores that fellowship with God, and that leads to good mental health.

6. How often this past year have you felt that God was with you?

When individuals first come to trust Christ as Savior, they sense that God is with them, that He is watching over them, and that He is going to take care of them. As time passes, sometimes that feeling fades and they forget that God is personally involved with them every day in every activity.

It is good for your mental health to realize and feel that God is present with you right now. If you've lost that feeling, make sure you talk with Him every day, through prayer, and that you allow Him to talk with you each day—through the Word, the prompting of His Holy Spirit, and the circumstances that He brings into your life. However, make sure that the latter two ways in which He speaks to you, which easily can be interpreted subjectively, according to our own desires, always agree with what He tells us through His written Word.

7. Can you pinpoint several instances this week in which you accomplished something "through Christ," as Paul proclaimed he did in Philippians 4:13?

"I can do all things through Christ which strengtheneth me" (KJV).

Amid the stresses of life, we must realize that our ability to do anything comes only "through Christ." In discussing the ups and downs of his experiences, Paul related all ability and achievement to the enabling of Christ. To live the Christian life apart from Christ's power is impossible. But to give over the responsibility of living the Christian life to divine power alone, apart from human responsibility, was never intended, either. That verse shows that divine enablement and human responsibility work hand in hand.

THE BURNOUT ESCAPE METHOD

Until you can put all the principles of chapters 8, 9, and 10 at work in your life (which will take time), you might memorize or carry with you this outline, to check how you are doing in escaping from burnout.

1. Use time wisely.
2. Keep priorities straight.
3. Relax more.
4. Realize I am someone in Christ.
5. Watch perfectionistic tendencies.
6. Look at the true meaning of life.
7. If truly suicidal, make immediate arrangements for hospitalization (through your doctor, pastor, or a nationally-recognized Christian therapy clinic).

Remember that your priorities start with those things that are eternal and, besides God Himself, only two things will last with you forever: the Word of God and your relationships with other Christians, including your family.

11
THE REKINDLING OF HOPE

When an individual experiences burnout, he or she invariably becomes "I" centered. In fact, many burnout victims sound like the prophet Jeremiah in Lamentations 3:16: "He has broken my teeth with gravel; he has trampled me in the dust." They may not always think that of God, but they will think it of some person in authority over them or of someone who is more powerful than they. We have been encouraged to see, however, that in our personal experience and in our ministry to others, redirecting our attention toward what God has for us, as manifested in His Word, can rekindle hope and help alleviate the symptoms of burnout.

One of the most common characteristics of advanced burnout is the loss of hope. Over recent years we have heard of hundreds of individuals, housewives, students, pastors, missionaries, lawyers, businessmen, accountants, executives, and others express the same thing: "I just don't feel that there's any hope of changing the situation."

Hope is an essential ingredient, we've observed, to withstanding the difficulties and pressures of life. The author of Hebrews refers to hope as "an anchor for the soul" (6:19). We see severe emotional traumas and disorders overcome, seemingly irreparable marital conflicts healed and homes restored, and one tragedy after another endured—but only when there is hope.

A Midwestern businessman recently told us of the tragedies that had marked him and his wife. First, his son was killed in a traffic accident. Soon thereafter a daughter took her life on Christmas Day. Within a matter of months, another son took his life. How could he and his wife survive? Certainly, they had grieved over their losses, but as this man expressed it, "We didn't lose hope. We believe our children have trusted Christ as their Savior. Even though tragedy took them from us, we will see them again." Can such hope really exist and not falter, even after such tragedy?

A SETTLED HOPE

The word for "hope" commonly used in Scripture does not mean a sense of wishing something were so. The biblical concept of hope is more of a settled anticipation, a "favorable and constant expectation."[1] The Greek verb form for "hope" used in the New Testament frequently is closely related to the concept of *trust* (John 5:45; 2 Corinthians 1:10). The noun form in the New Testament is frequently associated with the specific prospect of Christ's return to earth, as in Titus 2:13, "The blessed hope—the glorious appearing of our great God and Savior, Jesus Christ."

JEREMIAH: OUR MODEL FOR HOPE

One of the most extensive developments of the subject of hope occurs in the Old Testament, in Jeremiah's book of Lamentations. Here, set against the

1. W. E. Vine, *Expository Dictionary of New Testament Words* (Old Tappan, N.J.: Revell, 1966), p. 232.

backdrop of a nation facing disaster and ruin, a prophet whose eyes are saturated with tears discovers that his hope, which has been depleted and even obliterated by the tragic end of the nation, is rekindled and refocused in his God. The prophet Jeremiah's experiences, recorded in Lamentations 3, give practical suggestions for people today who have experienced burnout.

Most burnout victims can identify with the words of Jeremiah in Lamentations 3:1: "I am the man who has seen affliction by the rod of his wrath." Although Jeremiah is designated in that passage as a representative of the nation, he is nonetheless describing the personal sorrows he experienced under the hand of God. Verses 1-24 contain almost forty references to *I*, *me* or *my*. Notice the graphic terms, in verses 2-16, with which Jeremiah decribes his perception of the circumstances in which he finds himself.

> He has driven *me* away and made *me* walk
>   in darkness rather than light;
> indeed, he has turned his hand against *me*
>   again and again, all day long.
> He has made *my* skin and *my* flesh grow old
>   and has broken *my* bones.
> He has besieged *me* and surrounded *me*
>   with bitterness and hardship
> He has made *me* dwell in darkness
>   like those long dead.
> He has walled *me* in so *I* cannot escape;
>   he has weighed *me* down with chains.
> Even when *I* call out or cry for help,
>   he shuts out *my* prayer.
> He has barred *my* way with blocks of stone;
>   he has made *my* paths crooked.
> Like a bear lying in wait,
>   like a lion in hiding,
> he dragged *me* from the path and mangled *me*

and left *me* without help.
He drew his bow
  and made *me* the target for his arrows.
He pierced *my* heart
  with arrows from his quiver.
I became the laughing stock of all *my* people;
  they mock *me* in song all day long.
He has filled *me* with bitter herbs
  and sated *me* with gall.
He has broken *my* teeth with gravel;
  he has trampled *me* in the dust.

(Italics added)

HOPE EXHAUSTED

Certainly Jeremiah's language vividly describes what victims of burnout frequently feel, even in the way in which adversity is attributed to God or someone else more powerful than they.

Lamentations 3:17-19 summarizes what many victims of burnout feel.

I have been deprived of peace;
  I have forgotten what prosperity is.
So *I* say, "*My* splendor [strength] is gone
  and all that *I* had hoped from the Lord."
I remember *my* affliction and *my* wandering,
  the bitterness and the gall.

(Italics added)

The victim loses peace, prosperity, and strength. He gains misery, bitterness, and pain. That is a situation where hope has been exhausted.

HOPE REKINDLED

Against this "death of hope" backdrop, Jeremiah suddenly says, "Yet this I call to mind and therefore I have hope" (v. 21). It is as if Jeremiah spots a light in the distance, toward which he now focuses attention.

The word used here for "hope" is one most closely associated with the concept of waiting and carries the idea of an expectation, thus leading from faith, to trust, to patient waiting. The meaning of that kind of hope is not a pacifying wish of the imagination to drown out troubles, nor is it uncertain, wishful thinking. That kind of hope, instead, refers to a solid ground for expectation directed towards God.[2] The significance of that inward shift is obvious. Although the agony of his experiences brought hope to an end, it was rekindled when the prophet's mind was directed toward certain truths about God rather than toward his present circumstances.

HOPE REFOCUSED

Jeremiah then goes on to examine four significant truths in Lamentations 3:22-23. Notice that, by that time, his "I" outlook had changed considerably.

> Because of the Lord's great love *we* are not consumed.
>> for *his* [God's] compassions never fail.
> They are new every morning;
>> great is *your* faithfulness.

> (Italics added)

With hope rekindled and refocused:

1. *He examines God's great, loyal love.* The term *loyal love* is one of the most significant concepts in the Old Testament. It is a term used frequently of God's covenant relationship with his followers. Its parts include loyalty, love, and mercy (kindness or compassion). It is seen in God's relationship with Israel and with us (Psalm 85:7; 98:3).

2. R. Laird Harris, ed., *Theological Wordbook of the Old Testament,* vol. 1 (Chicago: Moody, 1980), p. 373.

The point Jeremiah is making is that those to whom he was writing (and by application, those of us who belong to God today), can count on God's loyalty, love, and mercy toward us, no matter how desperate our circumstances. Even in the midst of burnout, we can still look to God who is never unloving or disloyal to us. He will never stop loving us unconditionally.

2. *He observes God's compassion.* God not only is loyal and trustworthy, but He feels our emotions. He will never fail to be moved with kindness and compassion in His actions toward us.

3. *He realized God's compassionate concern is unending.* No matter how dark the day, they are "new every morning." They never grow old, wear out, or become obsolete. God is always loyal, loving, and compassionate.

4. *He knows, consequently, that God is greatly to be trusted.* As the apostle Paul also came to realize, God is sovereign and, because of that, all things can be counted on to "work together for good to them who love God, to them who are the called according to his purpose" (Romans 8:28, KJV).

During times of stress and burnout, we have found these truths to be fundamental in rekindling hope and alleviating the spiritual and emotional stresses of burnout. We personally have applied them, as did Jeremiah. "The Lord is my portion; therefore I will wait for him" (v. 24).

BURNOUT REVERSED

We have shared these words with countless individuals with positive results. Certainly, physical and emotional needs must be met, too, as in the case of Elijah, when God provided food and rest, encouragement, and comfort of a friend (such as Elisha). However, the essence of reversing burnout is expressed in Lamentations 3:24-26:

> I say to myself, "The Lord is my portion;
> therefore I will wait for him."
> The Lord is good to those whose hope is in him,
> to the one who seeks him;
> it is good to wait quietly
> for the salvation of the Lord.

Even though circumstances may have our "face in the dust" (v. 29), when we focus beyond our circumstances we will be able to say "I have hope." Although the characteristics of burnout may vary in intensity and combination, although they may be cyclical or progressive, although they may come over weeks, months, or even years—whatever the case—through focusing on God and hoping in Him, burnout can be reversed.

When the principles we have shared in this book are applied, particularly those in the spiritual realm, we have seen hundreds of people *regain* hope, *refocus* their perspective, *center* their attention on the Lord and on waiting for Him, and *renew* their strength.

It has been like music to our ears to hear men and women echo the words of David, "He restores my soul" (Psalm 23:3). We are convinced that by taking the initiative while depending on the Lord, you *can* beat burnout.

12
RECOVERY FROM BURNOUT

The term *burnout* is never found in Scripture. However, there are many biblical examples of people whose symptoms parallel those of today's burnout victims. When someone undergoes burnout, it involves the loss of two important elements from that person's life: strength and hope. The Bible gives many examples of individuals who lost those two important elements and who lost, as a result, much of their effectiveness in serving God. One of the most vivid of those, along with one of the most practical biblical prescriptions for overcoming the loss of strength and hope, is not given in an account of an individual, however, but of a nation—Israel. That account is found in Isaiah 40.

A major thrust of the Old Testament is the fact that God called Israel as a nation to be His representative in the world. During the glory days of the nation's deliverance from Egypt under Moses, the conquest of the Promised Land under Joshua, and the establishing of the kingdom of David and of his son, Solomon, the nation functioned as God's servant with a relatively strong degree of effectiveness.

However, by the time Isaiah appeared on the scene, the nation had experienced hundreds of years of spiritual indifference, misplaced priorities, compromise, and a lack of personal commitment to God.

Consequently, the law of sowing and reaping was in full operation. The ten northern tribes had been scattered by the Assyrians when the prophet Isaiah wrote the comforting words of Isaiah 40. He was seeking to prepare what was left of the nation for the impending disaster of captivity by the Babylonians.

We are not suggesting that the nation of Israel was a victim of burnout, but we do see a strong parallel between what occurred to Israel and their circumstances, to which Isaiah spoke, and the spiritual factors that frequently contribute to burnout today. When Christians neglect appropriate spiritual priorities, compromise biblical convictions, and allow their personal commitment to Jesus Christ to be weakened by such factors as personal pleasures, desire for material possessions, and efforts to achieve power and influence (1 John 2:15), the results will be a loss of spiritual strength, which ultimately can lead to a loss of hope.

That does not mean a Christian will ever find his salvation in jeopardy; it is secured by Christ's death on the cross, by the full payment for all our sins, including those we will commit as Christians. Israel was still God's chosen people, even though as a nation she was powerless to be an effective witness for God and even though her inhabitants felt hopeless in their circumstances.

Isaiah's message to Israel was designed to call the nation's attention to God, who alone can provide the physical, emotional, and spiritual healing necessary for those without hope or strength. It is significant that in Isaiah 40 the prophet spends the bulk of the chapter—through verse 26—pointing a spotlight toward Israel's God, showing Him to be both powerful (the Creator) and caring (The Shepherd).

Then, in verse 27, Isaiah lovingly confronts his people with their problem. He personifies Israel the nation as an individual suffering from attitudes generally present in what we now call burnout. They are feelings of isolation and of injustice.

The feeling of isolation is expressed by Isaiah's question to Israel, "Why do you say, O Jacob, and complain, O Israel, 'My way is hidden from the Lord' " (v. 27). In much the same way, today's burnout victim also feels isolated and unappreciated. He or she says, "Nobody appreciates me. No one understands me." Those thoughts relate to family, employer, fellow employees, teachers, friends, and others. The feeling of isolation often is most intense when the people closest to the burnout victim are involved.

Closely paralleling the feeling of isolation is the feeling of injustice. That is also reflected in Isaiah 40:27: "Why do you say, O Jacob, and complain, O Israel . . . my cause [rights] is disregarded by my God'?" All too often, today's exhausted burnout victim says, "It's just not fair!" That feeling can be related to family matters, studies, work, and even to successes enjoyed by friends.

After sharing those statements symptomatic of Israel's condition, Isaiah shifts the focus from what the nation says to what Israel actually has in the Lord. Again, a parallel can be made in the symptoms experienced by the nation and those experienced by the individual whose spiritual condition has brought on burnout today.

> He gives strength to the weary ["faint," KJV]
> and increases the power of the weak.
> Even youths grow tired and weary,
> and young men stumble and fall.
> (vv. 29-30)

Four significant characteristics, "faint," "weary," "weak," and "stumble and fall," are given in those words from Isaiah. Each of them can apply to those suffering from burnout today.

Faint. This term, used again at the end of the chapter, "and not be faint," describes one who is about to pass out from a lack of nourishment. Most of us have experienced times when we went many hours without proper nourishment and perhaps without rest. Today's burnout victim, because of long hours, inability to sleep, and perhaps poor eating habits tends perpetually to feel at the point of fainting.

Weary. An individual suffering from burnout is characterized by perpetual exhaustion. Like a rubber band stretched beyond its capacity, he or she has lost elasticity. A college student drove himself during two rigorous semesters of work, study, and ministry, climaxed by several all-night stints of study in preparation for exams. After staying up all night cramming the night before his most crucial exam, he fell asleep a half-hour before the exam was scheduled to begin. he slept through the exam, failed the course, and eventually dropped out of school. He suffered the consequences of his burnout.

Weak. The burnout victim suffers a drop in his concentration level and in his ability to produce. Since we often tend to judge people on their ability to produce, there is often a parallel drop in feelings of self-worth. The decline in the ability to concentrate often results from, and enhances, anxiety. In Matthew 6, our Savior three times commands. "Do not be anxious" (NASB). The term He uses in those three commands is a Greek word signifying division. The anxious individual has become distracted, divided in his attention. As a result he or she is unable to function at previous levels of efficiency.

Stumble and fall. The student who slept through his exam also illustrates a fourth significant characteristic that parallels those of today's burnout victims. The individual suffering from burnout is like an accident looking for a place to happen, to "stumble and fall." He is headed for a disaster—a blowup in a personal relationship, a physical collapse, or even a spiritual or moral failure. That individual is likely to crash unless his burnout is dealt with properly. Isaiah adds that even the youth of his day faced the possibility of major disaster without feeling how close they were to the brink. So it is with potential burnout victims today. Indeed, college age and other young, dedicated Christians are among the most likely to suffer from burnout and its devastating characteristics as they start out life on their own with all their might, not knowing their own limitations.

As Christina Maslach so aptly put it,

> Burnout—the word evokes images of a final, flickering flame; of a charred and empty shell; of dying embers and cold, gray ashes. . . . Once fired up about their involvement with other people—excited, full of energy, dedicated, willing to give tremendously of themselves for others . . . [burnout victims] did give . . . and give and give, until finally there was nothing left to give any more. The teapot was empty, the battery was drained, the circuit was overloaded—they had burned out.[1]

Despite the bleak picture painted in Isaiah 40, the prophet does hold out hope for those who were experiencing the symptoms brought on by the years of spiritual decline and failure in Israel. In verses 28-31, Isaiah presents the solution, which starts with this basic reminder:

1. Christina Maslach, *Burnout—The Cost of Caring* (Englewood Cliffs, N.J.: Prentice-Hall, 1982), p. 3.

Do you not know?
  Have you not heard?
The Lord is the everlasting God,
  the Creator of the ends of the earth.
He will not grow tired or weary,
  and his understanding no one can fathom.

It is marked by the character of a gift:

He gives strength to the weary
  and increases the power of the weak.

It is experienced by those who wait on the Lord.

But those who hope in [wait upon] the Lord
  will renew their strength.
They will soar on wings like eagles;
  they will run and not grow weary,
  they will walk and not be faint.

RECOVERY STARTS WITH A REMINDER

As in the case of many physical, emotional, and spiritual problems, the prophet Isaiah points out to Israel ("Do you not know? Have you not heard?") that the information necessary for solving their burnout problem is already at hand.

The prophet is doing what was needed for Israel then, which is the solution to the spiritual aspect of burnout today. He is refocusing attention from the nation to God, from the nation's inability to God's infinite ability. If a burnout victim is experiencing the following symptoms, he or she can profit greatly from applying the principles that Isaiah shared with God's weak and hopeless people of his day.

| The burnout victim is about to give up and feels the end has come. | The prophet presents God as everlasting. |

The burnout victim perceives self as forsaken by God and man.	The prophet presents God as "Yahweh," the covenant-keeping God.
The burnout victim perceives self as helpless.	The prophet presents God as Creator of the ends of the earth.
The burnout victim perceives self as at the point of fainting— utterly weary.	The prophet presents God as neither fainting from overexertion nor growing weary from overwork.
The burnout victim perceives self as confused, unable to figure out a solution to the dilemma.	The prophet presents God as possessing infinite understanding.

In many pastoral and clinical counseling situations, individuals experiencing burnout have come to feel and experience hope when their attention has been focused beyond their circumstances to the characteristics of the God they serve. Indeed, for the person who has placed personal trust in Jesus Christ, burnout is a problem that can be solved.

RECOVERY IS MARKED BY A GIFT

The second facet of Isaiah's solution, as it applies to modern burnout, is that by nature it is a gift. "He gives strength to the weary and increases the power of the weak." Just as salvation is a gift from God, received by His grace through faith, and it is in no way of ourselves (Ephesians 2:8-9), so the power and energy necessary to overcome burnout must be received as a gift from God.

RECOVERY IS EXPERIENCED BY WAITING

Finally, the prophet reaches the heart of his solution for Israel. He explains that renewal of strength and hope is experienced by those who "hope in [wait upon] the Lord" (v. 31). One of the primary irritations confronting us in our fast-paced society is waiting. We wait for elevators and traffic lights, find ourselves placed on hold and waiting when using the telephone, stand in line and wait at the checkout counter of grocery stores, sit and wait in reception rooms of doctors' and dentists' offices, and otherwise occupy a great deal of time just waiting. Few of us enjoy it. Many of us become extremely impatient and irritated when forced to wait.

Yet one of the most important, biblical principles found throughout the Bible involves waiting. A profitable study involves considering the Old and New Testament words for "wait" and the contexts in which they are used. Waiting is an important ingredient in our personal spiritual growth and development. It is designed by God to build into our lives a number of important traits. He uses waiting to produce such important fruits of the Spirit as longsuffering, meekness, and self-control. Throughout the Psalms, David makes frequent reference to the blessings that will befall those who wait on the Lord. In Lamentations 3, Jeremiah explains that "it is good to wait quietly for . . . the Lord."

The word used by Isaiah for "wait" is an illustrative Hebrew term describing a rope stretched taut. It is closely related to the term used for the scarlet thread, the cord hung from Rahab's home in Jericho in Joshua 2. The significance of that is that the waiting process is a stretching one, one that is often extremely difficult but one that ultimately has a good end.

Isaiah promises renewal of strength to those who

wait upon and hope in the Lord. Here he utilizes another vivid Old Testament term that is related, in its root meaning, to the concept of "passing through." It was used of a change of clothes and of a knife cutting or passing through meat or other material. A related term in Job 14:7 refers to the second growth of a tree that has been cut down.

The significance of that term to today's burnout victim is important. Like an old and battered car, the burnout victim's strength is depleted. He has been many miles and feels he cannot long continue on. The Lord's promise is that waiting on Him will bring renewal of strength. His old, faltering strength will be traded in for God's limitless energy. Physically, emotionally, and spiritually, he will become like new by waiting upon the Lord.

Waiting thus becomes an expression of trust in the God who is described by Jeremiah as being "good to those whose hope is in [who wait on] him" (Lamentations 3:25) and who, according to David, strengthens the heart of those who wait on Him (Psalm 27:14).

The picture of these Israelite individuals who were faint, powerless, weary, and experiencing complete disaster, now soaring as eagles, running long distances without growing weary, and walking without fainting, completes the description of a spiritual principle that, when applied today, provides a workable cure for the spiritual dimension of burnout.

Don't despair. There is hope! There is a solution available to the child of God. By turning attention away from self and one's seemingly hopeless, helpless condition and onto the everlasting God, the burnout victim can find strength renewed. By waiting on the Lord, he or she can find a constant supply of wisdom and strength from the God who faints not, who is never weary, and who Himself will never experience burnout!